# The Lean Healthcare Dictionary

An Illustrated Guide to Using the Language
of Lean Management in Healthcare

# The Lean Healthcare Dictionary

An Illustrated Guide to Using the Language
of Lean Management in Healthcare

## Rona Consulting Group

CRC Press
Taylor & Francis Group
Boca Raton  London  New York

CRC Press is an imprint of the
Taylor & Francis Group, an **informa** business

A PRODUCTIVITY PRESS BOOK

CRC Press
Taylor & Francis Group
6000 Broken Sound Parkway NW, Suite 300
Boca Raton, FL 33487-2742

© 2015 by Taylor & Francis Group, LLC
CRC Press is an imprint of Taylor & Francis Group, an Informa business

No claim to original U.S. Government works

Printed on acid-free paper
Version Date: 20141014

International Standard Book Number-13: 978-1-4822-3289-9 (Paperback)

### Library of Congress Cataloging-in-Publication Data

Lean speak for healthcare : the productivity improvement dictionary / Rona
Consulting.
p. ; cm.
Includes bibliographical references and index.
ISBN 978-1-4822-3289-9 (paperback : alk. paper)
I. Rona Consulting Group, issuing body.
[DNLM: 1.  Delivery of Health Care--Dictionary--English. 2.
Efficiency, Organizational--Dictionary--English. 3.  Health Services
Administration--Dictionary-English.  W 13]

RA423
362.103--dc23                                                              2014039481

**Visit the Taylor & Francis Web site at**
**http://www.taylorandfrancis.com**

**and the CRC Press Web site at**
**http://www.crcpress.com**

# Contents

# Preface

The principles of lean management and lean production, derived from the Toyota Production System, are at work today in just about every industry and type of organization—from automotive factory floors to hotels, from finance companies to nonprofit organizations, and in the clinical and support services of healthcare. In hospitals, emergency rooms, operating rooms, clinics, medical offices, and labs, lean principles are helping dedicated clinicians and administrators achieve high levels of quality, work toward "zero defects," assure patient safety, increase patient satisfaction, empower staff, and improve financial performance.

In healthcare, as in any other industry, lean practitioners must be able to translate and interpret lean principles in order to apply them effectively in their work and in their organizations. This compendium of lean and healthcare terms was created to help meet that need. It is designed for two broad audiences, who often come together during lean transformation initiatives:

- first, the healthcare executives, clinicians, and support staff who initiate, steer, and participate in the lean transformation process, and who need to be conversant in lean vocabulary and knowledgeable about essential lean principles; and

■ second, administrators and experienced lean practitioners who are relative newcomers to healthcare and require both a basic grasp of how to translate lean terms to the work of healthcare, as well as a quick reference to essential healthcare acronyms and terms that commonly arise when lean principles are applied in healthcare settings.

The content of this book is firmly rooted in the hands-on experience of Rona Consulting Group, whose principals have designed and led groundbreaking applications of lean management in emergency rooms, operating rooms, labs, hospitals, and major medical centers.

In addition, a variety of sources were used to compile terms and their definitions. *LeanSpeak: The Productivity Business Improvement Dictionary,* developed and published by Productivity Press in 2002, served as a primary source; we are grateful to the staff of the Productivity Development Team, whose expertise permeated that original volume. Definitions of lean terms have also been compiled from the growing list of books that comprise the Lean Tools for Healthcare series, by Rona Consulting Group and Productivity Press. Healthcare term definitions were derived largely from authoritative government sources, mainly public resources provided by the U.S. Department of Health and Human Services (HHS) and its operating divisions and agencies. We also acknowledge the work of Margaret F. Schulte, DBA, FACHE, CPHIMS, whose book *Healthcare Delivery in the U.S.A.: An Introduction, 2nd edition* (Productivity Press/CRC Press, 2013) was an invaluable resource. For a complete listing of sources and recommended reading, see the Appendix.

Special thanks to the individuals at Rona Consulting Group who contributed to compiling, reviewing, and editing this volume, including Thomas Jackson, who conceived and spearheaded the project, Dr. Samuel Carlson, Susie Creger, Steve Mattson, Mike Rona, and Ritsuko Sumii Travis. Heidi

Gehris-Butenschoen acted as coordinator and designed the cover concept. Thanks also to Maura May, who served as project manager and editor and who extended and expanded many of the definitions.

Finally, thanks to the doctors, nurses, technicians, administrators, and executives whose tireless work, probing questions, and commitment to quality healthcare in their organizations inspire us in our work every day.

# About the Author

**Rona Consulting Group** develops healthcare leaders who make things better for patients: safer care, higher quality, fewer waits, and lower costs.

Its mission is to transform healthcare leaders into lean executives who will, in turn, transform their organizations— helping clinicians and staff members pursue perfection in all of their organizational processes.

Based in Seattle, Washington, Rona Consulting Group is a lean consultancy serving the healthcare industry. Rona Consulting Group develops transformational leaders who are capable of educating and coaching their managers, clinicians, and support staff to become a lean healthcare organization. They are committed to helping healthcare organizations and purchasers of healthcare achieve the highest quality through zero defects, increased patient satisfaction, empowerment of staff, and improvement in financial performance through the application of the Toyota Management System.

# LEAN TERMS FOR HEALTHCARE

# 1

## 3P

*See* production preparation process.


## 4 Ms or 5 Ms

*See* five Ms.


## 5S

A disciplined approach to managing workplace organization of physical things and information to make it easy to identify errors, defects, abnormal conditions, and any other types of deviation from standard. The five S's are *sort, set in order, shine, standardize,* and *sustain*. (The Japanese words for these are *seiri, seiton, seiso, seiketsu,* and *shitsuke*.)


## 5 whys

*See* five whys.


## 80/20 rule

*See* Pareto principle.

# A

## A3

A type of management document and report printed on large format "A3" (Europe and Asia) or tabloid (the Americas) paper and used for planning, problem solving, and communication. In healthcare, A3 can also mean ensuring that clinicians and support staff hold each other accountable to provide access and appropriate care for their patients. For more on several variants of A3 reports, see A3i, A3P, A3T (with illustration: *See also* storyboard), A3SR, and A3X (with illustration).

## A3i

An A3 "intelligence" report that summarizes changes in competitive intelligence and presents ideas for a strategic response.

## A3P

An A3 "problem" report that is used in finding root causes and implementing countermeasures to major, unanticipated problems in patient safety, quality, delivery lead time, and cost.

## A3SR

An A3 "status report" that is used to track process improvements connected to targets established in an A3T.

**A**

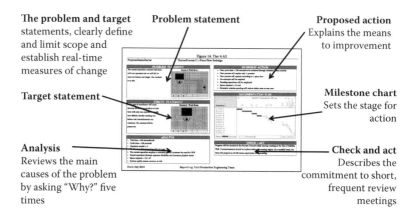

The problem and target statements, clearly define and limit scope and establish real-time measures of change

Problem statement

Proposed action
Explains the means to improvement

Target statement

Milestone chart
Sets the stage for action

Analysis
Reviews the main causes of the problem by asking "Why?" five times

Check and act
Describes the commitment to short, frequent review meetings

**Figure 1    A3 team charter (A3T).**

# A3T

An A3 "team charter" report that is used to circulate and build consensus around proposals for major improvements in patient safety, quality, delivery lead time, and cost during the strategic planning process. An A3T clearly links improvement activity to a significant problem and establishes definite targets and milestones. More than a project plan, it is a longer horizon roadmap (typically spanning 12–18 months) that represents a complete cycle of organizational learning. *See* Figure 1.

# A3 thinking

The rigorous application of the scientific method and genchi genbutsu involving frontline leaders and operators in formulating and testing hypotheses as part of a project defined by an A3T or A3P. *See also* plan-do-check-act (PDCA) cycle; lean thinking.

# A3X

**A**

An A3 "X-matrix" report that is a compilation of several A3Ts linked to a healthcare organization's overall strategy as well as to financial improvement targets; also known as a balanced scorecard. *See* Figure 2.

## abnormality

Any process or equipment condition that does not conform to the standard conditions required for the scheduled delivery of quality healthcare services.

## accountable

*See* RACI.

## activity board

A visual display used to communicate the activities and status of kaizen or other healthcare improvement projects and initiatives. *See* Figure 3.

## andon

A control device, usually a lighted display, used in a work area to alert staff to abnormalities and developing problems in quality, safety, or supply. Normally refers to a visual control, but can also be an audible or tactile signal. An alarm on an IV pump is an example of an andon device. An andon may also

A

**A3-X**

Legend

| | |
|---|---|
| ◉ | = strong correlation or team leader |
| ○ | = important correlation or core team member |
| △ | = weak correlation or rotating team member |
| ☐ | = no correlation or team membership |

**Accountability / Team members**
- President and CEO
- CMO
- Chief: primary care
- CNO
- Chief: medical specialties
- Chief: specialty services
- COO
- CFO
- Vice president of marketing
- Vice president of human resources
- Vice president of KPO
- Value stream manager: DRG 1
- Value stream manager: DRG 2
- Value stream manager: DRG 3

**Correlation / contribution**

*Growth*
- Decrease employee turnover by 5% by EOY.
- Train 10% of the workforce in PDCA3 by EOY.
- Complete lean enterprise basic training by EOY.
- % workforce devoted full time to Lean enterprise by EOY

*Process*
- Decrease process lead time by 15% by EOY.
- Increase process reliability by 15% by EOY.
- Increased outcome quality to 4.5 sigma by EOY

*Customer*
- Stream value to customers in one DRG by EOY.
- Increase patient satisfaction by 5% by EOY.
- Increase unique patients served by 5% by EOY.

**Tactics**
- Value stream initiative
- Primary care operations
- Inpatient care operations
- Medical specialty operations
- Specialty service operations
- Operations management department
- Finance department
- Marketing department
- Human resources department
- Kaizen promotion office

**Process Improvements**

**Strategic themes**
- Grow human resources.
- Build reliable processes.
- Create loyal customers.
- Decrease cost to sustain profitability.

**Financial results in $000**

| | year 1 | year 2 | year 3 | year 4 | year 5 |
|---|---|---|---|---|---|
| Revenue | $1,000 | $1,050 | $1,103 | $1,158 | $1,216 |
| Conversion cost | $100 | $98 | $97 | $96 | $95 |
| Direct cost | $800 | $785 | $771 | $757 | $743 |
| Value stream profit | $100 | $167 | $235 | $305 | $378 |
| Sustaining cost | $80 | $79 | $78 | $77 | $76 |
| EBITDA | $20 | $88 | $158 | $228 | $302 |
| Unique patients served | 400 | 420 | 441 | 463 | 486 |

© 2008 rona consulting group

rona consulting group

**Figure 2  A3 X-matrix report (A3X).**

**A**

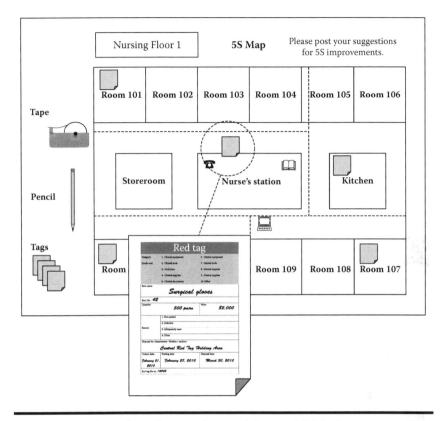

**Figure 3    Activity board example, used for a 5S initiative.**

be used to show the status of work in progress, and sometimes to provide work instructions (such as quality checks and equipment changes).

# andon cord

A hanging cord or other signaling device, immediately proximate to a work process, which a worker may pull to signal a problem in real time and temporarily halt work if the problem cannot be solved immediately.

## autonomation

The transfer of "human intelligence" to equipment or a process, such that any abnormality or defect produced is automatically detected and the machine or process is stopped; for example, a CT scanner that stops if it is lowered too close to a patient. Exposing abnormalities leads to prevention of mistakes, or "building in quality." *See also* jidoka.

## available time

The time scheduled for the delivery of healthcare services or other operations, less any amount of time those operations are closed because of scheduled lunches, dinners, breaks, meetings, and so on. Available time is a factor used to calculate takt time.

## average demand

The mean of historical patient or customer demand for a period (a day, a shift, or other discrete time period) for which you are calculating takt time.

# B

## balance chart

An operator balance chart. *See* percent load chart.

## balanced scorecard

A measurement system that enables a healthcare organization to clarify its vision and strategy and translate them into action. By balancing metrics against the intent of the plan, it helps an organization weigh financial and nonfinancial impacts and establish lean performance measurables. Key areas often assessed include patient/customer relations, financial management, internal business processes, employee performance, quality, safety, organizational learning, and innovation. *See also* A3X.

## batch-and-queue production

A non-lean process in which all the patients or units in a given lot complete a particular stage of production before moving to the next stage. This creates a "batch" of patients or service units, which then wait in a "queue" or line at each stage while each is processed in turn. Contrast with continuous flow production.

## benchmarking

The search for industry best practices that lead to superior performance (*See* Robert Camp, *Benchmarking,* Productivity Press, 2006, p. 12). Benchmarking is a formal process through which healthcare organizations can identify best practices by looking at other internal operations and processes, at other healthcare organizations, at similar functional processes in other companies (e.g., an inpatient discharge process at another hospital), or generically (i.e., by looking at best practices in seemingly unrelated areas and identifying parallels and breakthrough ideas).

## bottleneck

The point in a process that adversely affects throughput. As a resource capacity limitation, a bottleneck will not allow a system to flow and meet the demand of the patient or customer. *See also* constraint.

## brownfield

An existing facility or process operating by established methods and systems, and in which lean methods and best practices can be applied to create new, waste-free processes. Contrast with greenfield.

## buffer

A stock or supply of finished goods available within the healthcare value stream so that takt time can be met when there are variations in patient or customer demand. In clinical situations, a buffer can mean a number of appropriately staffed and stocked exam rooms, beds, and other venues of care where patients are asked to wait a short, predetermined length of time under the appropriate level of care before moving to the next operation in the process. Buffers differ from FIFO lanes in that the patients in a buffer may or may not be served in the same order in which they arrived.

# C

## capacity planning

The process of predicting if and when system saturation will occur. This includes determining the maximum work load and throughput, how the work load will evolve, and the desired performance levels. Capacity management involves planning enhancements to the current system and evaluating the design of new systems.

## catchball

A give-and-take activity performed between different levels of a healthcare organization, to ensure the exchange of critical information and feedback on goals and objectives and to assess their feasibility. Catchball is a discrete phase of the hoshin kanri or policy management process, in which leaders deploy strategies and budgets to managers, and managers respond with their interpretation of expectations and any suggested changes. Catchball ensures that all levels are aligned in direction, strategy, implementation, assessment, measurement, and resources.

## cause-and-effect diagram

A diagram used to analyze the contributing factors or causes of a specific event, problem, or outcome. It is also called a *fishbone diagram* because it is shaped like a fish skeleton, where the "bones" of the fish represent various categories used to group causes (typically the five Ms.)

**C**

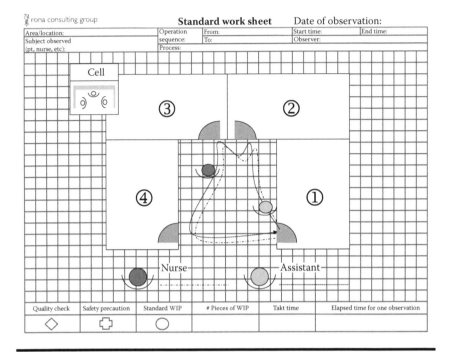

Figure 4   Diagram of a nursing cell.

# cell

A physical layout in which equipment and workers are aligned in the exact sequence needed to process a family of services, or where functional tasks are co-located and sequenced to optimize flow. In healthcare, a clinical cell is such an arrangement of clinical staff, equipment, medicines, and supplies, all in a single space, with the capability of producing healthcare services at takt time for patients without waiting between the various tasks and handoffs that define the operation. *See* Figure 4.

# chaku-chaku

A one-piece flow method used in a cell, in which a single operator moves from process to process or machine to machine taking the part or product just processed to the next machine or process without any effort required to unload processed parts. It depends on many other lean concepts being in place, such as heijunka, poka yoke, and the water strider. The term means "load-load" in Japanese.

**C**

# changeover

*See* setup.

# clinical cell

*See* cell.

# clinical value stream

The sequence of clinical processes required to provide integrated medical care to a patient with a specific illness, including the diagnostic processes necessary to determine the requirements of the patient's care plan and the clinical service-production processes by which the care plan is executed. *See also* value stream; value stream map.

# coach

A team builder, mentor, and role model for lean improvement groups within a healthcare organization.

# common cause variation

Variation attributable to the sum of many real but small causes that are inherent in—and part of—any process. There is no assignable root cause for common cause variation; reducing it requires the development of new processes and systems (see PDCA). Also known as *random variation*.

## compliance

An indication, judgment, or state in which an activity, product, service, or document meets the specifications or regulations set for it.

## constraint

Any operation in a process that cannot meet takt time or that is so critical to a process that any problem in it disrupts flow both upstream and downstream. In healthcare, highly skilled individuals, such as doctors or RNs, are frequently constraints partly because of their relatively high cost. Constraints can back up production, causing patients to wait for lengthy, often unpredictable amounts of time. A constraint has the lowest output rate when compared to the balance of other operations in a process. There is normally only one constraint at a time in a process sequence. Constraints typically fall into four types: physical (a bottleneck), logistical (e.g., response time), managerial (policies and rules), and behavioral (the activities of clinicians or other staff). *See also* bottleneck.

## consulting

*See* RACI.

## continuous flow production

A production system in which each patient, service unit, or product moves through its transformational cycles continuously, with no waits or delays. In clinical environments, the production and delivery of healthcare services to patients in a first-in-first-out order with zero waits between tasks and operations in the process. Contrast with batch-and-queue production.

**C**

## continuous improvement

*See* kaizen.

## control chart

A chart using statistical process control principles to determine if a system or process is in statistical control and the types of variation affecting it. Control charts graph randomly selected data points over time, and show whether variation in the process is common cause variation (inherent in the system) or special cause variation (a specific cause that can be addressed).

## corrective action

Action carried out to correct a noncompliance. *See also* compliance.

## countermeasure

An improvement action taken to offset or respond to a problem, ideally targeting the root cause to prevent recurrence. In the spirit of PDCA experimentation and kaizen, countermeasures are put in place to be tested and, if successful, used until future improvement cycles reveal even better countermeasures.

The term countermeasure is preferred to "solution," which implies the discovery of a final answer.

## cross-functional team

A team composed of representatives from several functional areas in a healthcare organization.

## C/T

*See* cycle time.

## current state map

A value stream map that shows the essential operations of a healthcare process as currently performed; the map is then used to identify systematically which activities are value-added in the eyes of the patient or other customer, and which are considered waste. *See also* future state map; value stream map.

## customer

Someone for whom a product is made or a service performed. In healthcare, as in any organization, there are multiple internal and external customers. The *external customer* is the end user of a product, service, or information, for example the patient, patient's family, and payers. The *internal customer* is the downstream recipient of a clinician's, technician's, or staff member's work within the healthcare organization, for example an emergency room physician who receives a radiology lab report.

## customer focus

Attention to the customer's definition of value and criteria for services or products. Measuring the healthcare enterprise's success according to the level of patient or customer satisfaction rather than other internally focused performance measures.

**C**

## cycle time (C/T)

The time required for a single clinician or staff member to complete one cycle of operation in a process (e.g., admit, test, or treat) by following the standardized step sequence, including both value-added and non-value-added activities. It is also how often we should expect to see a patient, product, or service unit exiting an operation in a process.

# D

## daily management

A set of management routines built around visible standards in the workplace and PDCA cycles of improvement that happen at the front line when standards are not being met. All levels of leadership hold the next level accountable by practicing kata (improvement) questions in the gemba.

## defect

A non-conformance or departure from expected quality. In mistake-proofing terminology, a defect is not the same as an error; it is the result of an equipment malfunction or uncorrected human mistake or error that has been passed on undetected from one operator or process to the next.

## demand

The amount of products or services that patients or other customers need, and when they need them. Customer demand and available time for production are the two elements needed to determine takt time.

## Deming cycle

*See* plan-do-check-act (PDCA) cycle.

# downtime

Production time that is not usable because of equipment problems, lack of materials, lack of necessary information, or the unavailability of clinicians, staff, or other operators.

**D**

# E

## error

Something done incorrectly through a misunderstanding or as a result of an unreliable or unstable process, and not corrected. An error is likely to occur when any of the conditions necessary for successful processing are wrong or absent. The resulting departure from correct performance causes a defect. Note that in mistake-proofing terminology, an error is not the same as a defect.

## error proofing

*See* mistake proofing.

## executive sponsor

The leader (or leadership team representative) who initiates lean or kaizen initiatives in a healthcare organization, and who supports other leaders and teams in lean transformation efforts by clearing obstacles and providing access to resources. Also, the leader of a critical initiative or project defined through hoshin kanri.

## external customer

*See* customer.

## external setup

*See* setup.

# F

## failure mode and effects analysis (FMEA)

The systematic analysis of a product or service in its planning, design, and production stages to ensure that its potential and logical failures are relatively uneventful; that is, the root causes behind mistakes are found and fixed so as to prevent recurrence before the product or service is ever used by a patient or customer. The object of FMEA is to foresee and predict the frequency and severity of potential failure.

## feeder line

A production line that produces sub-assemblies of parts or subsets of services to feed the main production line, with the purpose of reducing variation on the main line.

## FIFO

An acronym for "first-in-first-out," FIFO refers to well-regulated, short queues in which all patients are cared for, or inputs processed, in the same order in which they originally lined up. The principle can also be used in inventory management to ensure that the oldest inventory is used first.

## FIFO lane

A short queue, positioned after the completion of an upstream operation, in which patients wait only a short, predetermined time before they are passed one at a time to a downstream operation or process.

## first in first out

*See* FIFO.

## five Ms

Five words starting with "M" that describe the five key areas of production in which quality problems can appear: man (people), machine (equipment), materials, and methods (process)—the original *4Ms*—plus mother nature, or milieu (the environment). These are useful when searching for root causes of problems, and are often used to form the "bones" of a cause-and-effect or fishbone diagram. There are variants on the five Ms; it is sometimes expanded to the *6 Ms* with the inclusion of measurement.

## five S

*See* 5S.

## five whys

A method of asking why five times when a problem is discovered to get to root cause and develop countermeasures.

## flow

Tasks achieved along a value stream so that a patient, service, product, or information moves from start to finish continuously, with no waits, delays, or defects. *See also* continuous flow production.

## flow manager

Team member located at the pacemaker process who is responsible for managing the sequence of patients and the pace and content of operator work to meet takt time.

## flow production

*See* flow; continuous flow production.

## FMEA

*See* failure mode and effects analysis.

## future state map

A value stream map depicting a process previously rendered in a current state map, but with the waste removed. Future state maps help healthcare teams envision dramatic improvements, plan them using the ideal state as a basis, and dislodge old patterns of thinking about their organizations and their respective roles within them. *See also* current state map; value stream map.

# G

## gemba or genba

The place where the actual work is performed—e.g., the clinic, the lab, the emergency room, the billing office; the "shop floor."

## gemba walk

A form of "leadership rounds," through which senior leaders, managers, and/or supervisors support continuous improvement and process standardization while ensuring that the efforts of all teams are aligned. Effective gemba walks are prepared for in advance and performed regularly. They involve careful observation, asking questions, listening actively for barriers and successes, coaching through Socratic methods, and assessing the need for any leadership countermeasures. Gemba walks are a part of leader standard work.

## genchi genbutsu

A method of empirical observation that involves going to the actual place where the real work happens to see it for oneself.

## genjitsu

The fact or reality, learned by personally observing work.

## go/no-go

A device, visual cue, or method that facilitates making a quick and accurate decision (at a glance or with one touch) as to whether a piece of equipment or point in the process meets a specific criterion, so that the process can proceed reliably.

## greenfield

**G**

A new system or space for which there is no pre-existing process or facility and in which lean methods and best practices can be used to design a waste-free process. Contrast with brownfield.

# H

## hansei

A process of introspective, critical self-reflection on both successes and failures along with commitment to improve based on that reflection.

## heijunka

A level production schedule that smoothes day-to-day variation and balances capacity with demand. *See also* level loading.

## heijunka box

A scheduling device used to spread production of services evenly throughout the day. The box visually displays each service family in a separate horizontal row, and is divided vertically into slots representing time intervals, or pitch increments. The slots are loaded with kanban that represent patient or customer services required. *See* Figure 5.

|  | 8:00–11:00 | 11:00–2:00 | 2:00–5:00 | 5:00–8:00 |
|---|---|---|---|---|
| Floor 1 | 1 | 5 | 9 | 1 3 |
| Floor 2 | 1 7 | 2 1 | 2 5 | 2 9 |
| Floor 3 | 3 3 | 3 7 | 4 1 | 4 5 |
| Floor 4 (maternity) | 4 9 | 5 3 | 5 7 | 6 1 |

**Figure 5    Heijunka box.**

# hoshin

A Japanese term meaning "compass," used to denote a strategic focus or direction.

# hoshin kanri

Literally, the management of a hoshin, also referred to as hoshin management or *policy deployment.* A strategic decision-making and deployment methodology used by a healthcare organization's executive team in order to focus resources keenly on the select few critical initiatives needed to accomplish organizational objectives. Using visual matrix diagrams, generally three to five key objectives are selected, refined, and deployed using a cascading, give-and-take communication process (catchball) between executive management and other levels. Resources are aligned throughout the organization, with measurable targets toward the key objectives that are reported on a regular basis. Hoshin kanri resolves large-scale projects into multiple, smaller projects, each with its own project manager or executive sponsor. Each project is documented by means of a project plan called an A3 or A3T. *See also* A3x and Figure 2.

# house of quality

A decision-making matrix shaped like a house that is used in the quality function deployment process as a tool for translating patient or customer requirements and expectations into the appropriate characteristics of a product or service. It helps a cross-functional project team weigh quality levels, customer expectations, benchmark data, target values, technical requirements, and production and delivery parameters.

# I

## informed

*See* RACI.

## internal customer

*See* customer.

## internal setup

*See* setup.

## inventory

All physical goods on hand that are to be consumed or transformed into a product or service. This includes "information in process" and "decisions in process." Inventory can mask inefficiencies.

# J

## jidoka

One of the two pillars of the Toyota Production System, using a combination of human intelligence and technology to automatically stop any process at the first sign of abnormality. *See also* autonomation.

## JIT

See just in time.

## just in time (JIT)

A phrase meaning "having available just what is needed, exactly where it is needed, when it is needed, and in just the right quantity." One of the two pillars of the Toyota Production System.

## just-in-time (JIT) production system

A production system in which either goods or services are delivered where they are needed, just in time to be used, and in the right quantities with only the amount of inventory needed to cope with known variability in supply and demand.

## just-in-time (JIT) purchasing system

A materials management system using small lot purchases with frequent delivery just in time for use, with suppliers chosen based on delivery, performance, and price.

# K

## kaikaku

Radical improvement or complete redesign of a process to improve functionality and eliminate waste. Contrast with kaizen, which is incremental improvement to an existing process.

## kaizen

Gradual, unending improvement, often translated as "continuous improvement." "Kai" means to change, and "zen" means good, or better; therefore kaizen is most literally "change to make better." Kaizen is based on the fundamentals of scientific analysis in which you analyze (or take apart) the elements of a process or system to understand how it works, and then discover how to influence or improve it (make it better).

## kaizen blitz

*See* kaizen workshop.

## kaizen event

A structured team activity aimed at eliminating waste, with a narrower focus and shorter timeframe than that of a kaizen workshop. The activities undertaken during a kaizen event might be focused on implementing a known solution or on implementing standard work in a new area.

## kaizen workshop

A team activity aimed at rapid use of lean methods to eliminate waste in particular areas of the healthcare organization. It is well planned and highly structured, typically over the course of five days, to enable quick, focused discovery of root causes and implementation of solutions.

## kakushin

Innovation, reform, or renewal; more fundamental than the incremental change of kaizen.

**K**

## kamishibai

A centuries-old form of instructive storytelling used in Japanese Buddhist temples (literally "picture-story show" or "paper drama"), the concept has been adapted as a type of visual management system. *Kamishibai boards* are used to display cards that show standard work, safety checks, or other tasks that need to be performed. The system can be used to show the status of work at a glance, and/or as a tool to be used in successive or "layered" process audits. Kamishibai boards are also used in leader standard work to visually represent, hour-by-hour, the daily and monthly management commitments of frontline managers, middle managers, and senior leaders. Each manager or leader is supposed to commit a particular percentage of his/her time to being on the gemba (the place where actual work is performed). As such, kamishibai boards promote the practice of genchi genbutsu or "going to see." *See also* storyboard.

# kanban

Any type of signal used by downstream processes to communicate readiness for production to upstream processes, and to trigger movement, production, or restocking. Literally "signal" or "signboard," kanban are usually in the form of a card, but may be a container, a token, or an electronic signal. In materials management systems, kanban are also used to signal the need for more materials, medicines, and supplies.

# kanban system

Likened to an autonomic nervous system for pull production, the kanban system controls the amount and movement of inventory and sometimes of patients, authorizes the production of services, provides visual control of operations and processes, and promotes improvement of healthcare service production. The kanban system is a critical element in a just-in-time production system.

**K**

# kata

Originally from the martial arts, a term applied in lean management contexts to represent the regular practice of maneuvers that become automatic and reflexive, and that allows free thinking and creativity to occur. In improvement work, it means thinking and behaviors that are so deeply ingrained that they become habits of improvement—a type of "second nature."

# key performance indicator (KPI)

A tracking and monitoring index of the progress of daily management systems.

# kit

A group of parts or supplies required for a single process (such as a surgical procedure), pregrouped together and provided by a single supplier, and delivered to the point of use at the time needed.

# KPI

*See* key performance indicator.

**K**

# L

## leader standard work

Structured work and routines that help healthcare leaders, managers, and supervisors shift to and maintain a focus on process as well as results; that provide consistency across the organization and during leadership transitions; and that reinforce standard work at all levels of the organization. May include activities such as accountability meetings, coverage of visual controls, work on improvements, training and mentoring, and regular gemba walks.

## lead time

The total amount of time required to produce a product or service for a patient or customer, from the time the customer initiates a request for service or orders a product (demand) until the request is fully completed (demand met and, in the case of total lead time, paid for), including all work cycle times and wait times. Stated another way, the time it takes for a single patient to move all the way through a process or an entire healthcare value stream from start to finish; for example, in the process of visiting a hospital, the lead time extends from the time the patient is admitted until the time of discharge (i.e., length of stay). The lead time for processing a urine sample extends from the time a doctor writes an order for the sample to be analyzed until the doctor receives results from the lab. Lead time and throughput time are the same when a scheduling and production system are running at or below capacity; lead time exceeds throughput time when demand exceeds capacity and additional waiting time is needed before the start of scheduling and production.

# lean

Without **muda** or "waste"; a shorthand term referring to the lean production system, of which the Toyota Production System is the foremost example.

# lean healthcare

Healthcare transformed by the principles of the Toyota Production System and Toyota Management System.

# lean management

The decentralized organization of management control structures to promote the discovery, correction, anticipation, and prevention of process defects and the errors and abnormalities that result in defects. The five principles of lean management are standard work, autonomation, flow production, PDCA, and the Socratic method.

# lean production

A strategy for the just-in-time production of products and services and the elimination of non-value-adding activities (wastes) from processes and value streams by involving all clinicians and other staff members and employees of a health-care organization in continuous improvement. A lean production system effectively optimizes the interactions among people, materials, and machines through elements such as standard work, kanban, visual display, one-piece flow, and the pull system, to provide high-quality products and services that are responsive to patient and customer needs.

# lean thinking

Thinking in terms of the Toyota Production System and Toyota Management System.

# level loading or level scheduling

Redistribution of work to ensure that clinicians and support staff utilize their respective skill sets to the highest level of their licensure, that idle time does not occur, and that no clinician or staff member is doing either too much or too little. *See also* heijunka.

# life-cycle cost

The total cost of a piece of equipment throughout its life, including design, manufacture, operation, maintenance, and disposal.

**L**

# line balancing

Balancing the assignment of tasks among workers so that the number of people working on a "line" or set of processes and the total amount of idle time are minimized and can meet takt time. *See also* percent load chart.

# Little's Law

Developed by John Little, the principle that the throughput of any system in a given period of time is equal to the work in process divided by lead time. For example, the number of patients discharged from a clinic over a certain period of time will always equal the number of patients currently in the clinic divided by the normal time it takes one patient (from arrival to discharge) to go through an entire visit to the clinic.

## lot production

Producing services or products in quantities larger than one, as opposed to one-piece flow. *See also* batch and queue.

## L/T

*See* lead time.

L

# M

## matrix diagram

A tool used to chart the relationships between elements in a situation or event. Elements are arranged in rows and columns on a chart. Symbols are placed at intersection points to show the presence or absence of a relationship between each pair of elements. *See*, for example, the matrix diagrams incorporated into the A3X-matrix report in Figure 2.

## maturity model

A model of the maturity level of an organization as it proceeds in its lean transformation. Maturity models allow the assessment of an organization against clear measures and benchmarks of best practices. The lean development criteria of the Shingo Prize (http://www.shingoprize.org/model) and the Transformation Ruler (see Thomas L. Jackson, *Hoshin Kanri for the Lean Enterprise*, Portland, OR: Productivity Press, 2006, Chapter 7) are good examples of maturity models.

## mentor

In a lean organization, leaders at different levels ideally function as mentors, or Socratic teachers, of the technical and social aspects of lean transformation, and they serve as role models for the healthcare organization's philosophy.

## mistake

*See* error.

| Before Induction | | | Before Incision | | | Before Wheels Out | | |
|---|---|---|---|---|---|---|---|---|
| **Key Participants** | | | | | | | | |
| **Nurse and Anesthetist** | | | **Nurse, Anesthetist, Surgeon** | | | **Nurse, Anesthetist, Surgeon** | | |
| | **Yes** | **No** | | **Yes** | **No** | | | |
| Identity confirmed? | √ | | Team members confirmed? | √ | | **Nurse** | **Yes** | **No** |
| Site marked? | √ | | Patient name, procedure, site confirmed? | √ | | Name of procedure? | √ | |
| Machine and meds okay? | √ | | | **Yes** | **No** | Instrument, sponge and needle counts okay? | √ | |
| Pulse oximeter functioning? | √ | | Antibiotic prophylaxis given in last 60 minutes? | √ | | | | |
| Known allergy? | | √ | | **Yes** | **No** | Specimen labeling? | √ | |
| Airway or aspiration risk? | | √ | Essential imaging displayed? | √ | | **Surgeon, Anesthetist, Nurse** | | |
| Risk of >500ml blood loss? | | √ | **Surgeon** | **Yes** | **No** | | **Yes** | **No** |
| Notes: | | | Critical or non-routine steps? | | √ | Key concerns for recovery? | | √ |
| | | | How long will the case take? | 120 min | | Notes: | | |
| | | | Anticipated blood loss? | <500 ml | | | | |
| | | | **Anesthetist** | **Yes** | **No** | | | |
| | | | Patient-specific concerns? | | √ | | | |
| | | | **Nurses** | **Yes** | **No** | | | |
| | | | Sterility confirmed? | √ | | | | |
| | | | Equipment issues/concern? | | √ | | | |

**M**

**Figure 6   Mistake-proofing example, a surgical safety checklist. (Adapted from the World Health Organization's 2009 "Surgical Safety Checklist." See http://www.who.int/patientsafety/safesurgery/tools_resources/en/.)**

# mistake proofing

A system for designing mechanisms or process devices or methods to make errors, or mistakes, impossible and to prevent defects. Examples of mistake-proofing devices and techniques include a color-coded wristband identifying a patient who is at risk for a fall; a medical gas outlet designed so that only the proper valve will fit; or a surgical safety checklist. *See* Figure 6.

# mixed model production

An approach in which quick changeover allows production of different products or services (e.g., surgeries or patient visits) in lot sizes approaching one through a single production line. Production is therefore more responsive to patient or customer needs that change quickly.

## mizusumashi

*See* water strider.

## monument

A piece of equipment imposing a constraint due to cost, size, immobility, or other factors that prevent a patient, service, or product from moving continuously.

**M**

## muda

Waste, or anything that consumes resources, adding cost or time, but creates no value; i.e., anything inconsistent with what the patient or customer requires. The key to lean healthcare is the total elimination of waste. *See also* seven wastes.

## mura

The waste of unevenness or inconsistency (in operations or processes).

## muri

The waste of overburden (e.g., "overloading" operators or equipment).

# N

## Nolan model

An improvement model based on the PDCA cycle, with the addition of three fundamental questions for improvement that address aims, measures, and ideas: (1) What are we trying to accomplish? (2) How will we know that a change is an improvement? (3) What changes can we make that will result in the improvements we seek?

## non-value-added time

The difference between the cycle time and the value-added time in a process or value stream. Non-value-added time results from any operation or activity that takes time and resources but does not add value to a product or service; it can be categorized in terms of the seven wastes.

N

# O

## Ohno, Taiichi

Japanese business leader and Toyota executive credited with developing the Toyota Production System. Also considered by some to be the "father" of the kanban system as a result of his observation of supermarket operations on a visit to the U.S. in 1956 and his subsequent work regarding continuous supply of materials to supermarket shelves.

## "one less" process

Continuously learning how to satisfy your patient or customer with "one less" unit of work in process or inventory in the pipeline, while improving quality, delivery, and cost.

## one-piece flow production

An element of the just-in-time production system, whereby processes flow continuously without waiting between various operations; processing equipment and locations are usually physically grouped together to ease process flow and minimize handoffs, or to allow one person to perform all the steps necessary to complete the process. *See also* cell.

## one-point lesson

A short, focused visual presentation that shares just-in-time information to improve performance. Information is presented in small chunks, when and where it is needed. Also called a *single-point lesson*, it can be used to fill basic knowledge gaps; to teach how to prevent process breakdowns, defects, or other abnormalities from recurring; or to summarize the results of a team improvement activity.

## operation

A specific sequence of tasks performed on a product or for a patient by a single machine or person (for example, the set of tasks a circulating nurse performs during a surgical procedure). A series of operations comprises a process.

## operator

The person who performs a task or operation, irrespective of their position or level in the organization. In healthcare, for example, this could be a doctor, nurse, technician, therapist, administrator, or billing specialist.

## operator balance chart

*See* percent load chart.

# P

## pacemaker

The one operation in a lean healthcare value stream that sets the standard pace of healthcare service production (based on takt time) for all upstream processes, so that the production of services can be synchronized. The pacemaker will always be the last process in the value stream where the order of production routinely needs to be reshuffled or rearranged by a flow manager; for example, the discharge process in a hospital.

## Pareto chart or diagram

A bar graph that draws on the Pareto principle and is used to identify and display the "critical few" versus the "trivial many" causes of a problem. Pareto analysis helps in determining the major causes of a problem by ranking them according to their relative contributions to the effect. The chart arranges bars representing the magnitude or frequency of each differ- ent cause identified from left to right in descending order. The cumulative percentage of the causes' contribution to the prob- lem is tracked by a line graph superimposed on the bar graph. *See* Figure 7.

## Pareto principle

Named after Italian economist Vilfredo Pareto, this principle states that 80 percent of an observed effect is usually due to roughly 20 percent of the observed causes. Also known as the

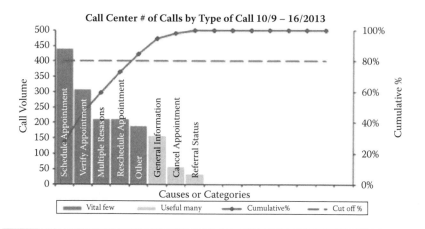

**Figure 7 Pareto chart or diagram.**

*80-20 rule,* it is a general principle of concentration, inequality, and inverse proportion. This principle reminds us that the relationship between inputs and outputs is not balanced and calls out disproportions so that corrective actions can be taken.

## patient-oriented layout

**P**

A layout geared to the production of healthcare services in which clinicians, staff, and equipment are arranged sequentially to facilitate quick and safe care for each patient.

## PDCA

*See* plan-do-check-act cycle.

## PDSA

An acronym for plan-do-study-act, another name for plan-do-check-act.

# percent load chart

A chart that makes visual the information from a time observation sheet (that is, the activities of work, including walking, for a specific operator relative to one patient). The chart is used to assess value-added versus non-value-added time; to eliminate waste; to determine how many clinicians and support staff are needed in each work area; and potentially to redistribute work so that takt time can be met (see line balancing). One of the five classic forms used for standard work documentation. Also known as an *operator balance chart. See* Figure 8.

# perfection

The complete elimination of waste (muda) so that all activities along a value stream create value.

# pitch

A scheduling increment that is based on takt time but provides a longer, more practical timeframe that allows the flow manager to determine whether the process is producing according to takt time. For example, if takt time for processing claims in an administrative office is 45 seconds, a pitch interval of one hour might be chosen. In each pitch interval, 80 claims need to be processed to meet demand consistently. (60 minutes = 3600 seconds. 3600 seconds ÷ 45 seconds/claim = 80 claims).

**P**

# plan-do-check-act (PDCA) cycle

An application of the scientific method to evaluate the effectiveness of tests of change (theories and ideas) in a set of four cyclical phases. *Plan*—evaluate the current situation, propose and

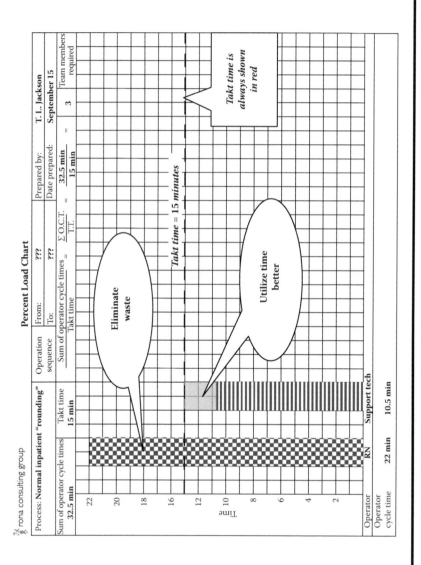

**Figure 8  Percent load chart.**

plan an idea or test for improving it, and state the hypothesis or expected outcome of the plan or test. *Do*—run the test and collect data. *Check* (sometimes called *Study*)—evaluate results and compare them to stated expectations. *Act*—if results of the Check (or Study) phase confirm expected outcomes, the test is a success; refine/enhance testing, and start the cycle again at Plan. If results do not confirm expected outcomes, start again at Plan to create new hypotheses and tests. Commonly referred to as *PDCA,* the plan-do-check-act cycle is also referred to as the *Shewhart cycle* after Walter Shewhart, the Bell Laboratories scientist who developed it, or the *Deming cycle* after W. Edwards Deming, a quality expert who collaborated with Shewhart. (Deming himself referred to it as the *Shewhart cycle.*)

## poka-yoke

Japanese term for mistake proofing. Also refers to a mistake-proofing device or defect-prevention method that usually includes a physical mechanism to ensure prevention.

P

## policy and objectives matrix

*See* P/O matrix.

## policy deployment

*See* hoshin kanri.

## P/O matrix

An A3X or X-type matrix used for strategic planning that shows organizational policies (strategies/goals), objectives (initiatives/projects), measures (targets/milestones), responsible party (teams/individuals/departments), impact on the organization (cost/benefit, financial/non-financial), and the relationship between each of these factors. This is all done on one large piece of paper. Also called *planning and objectives matrix*. For example, see Figure 2.

# P-Q analysis

*See* product–quantity analysis.

# president's diagnosis

An evaluative process used by top management to assess every aspect of the healthcare organization's status in relation to a maturity model or the adoption of best practices. A diagnosis can be distinguished from an audit in that an audit is often judgmental and carried out by an independent party, while a diagnosis is always helpful, carried out by a coach, and leads to prescribed countermeasures.

# process

A series of individual operations, performed for a patient or on a product, that transforms that patient or product from one state to another (for example, a surgical procedure). A process has inputs and outputs, and can transform a patient from "not vaccinated" to "vaccinated" or "not assessed" to "assessed," or a product from "not assembled" to "assembled."

# processing time

The time a patient is actually being cared for or product or service worked on. Typically a small fraction of lead time.

# process mapping

A visual means of understanding individual activities and operations and how they flow within the context of an entire process. Process maps can illustrate a single process or link cross-functional processes.

# process owner

Normally a department manager, the person who takes responsibility for choosing appropriate areas on which to focus attention in a kaizen event or kaizen workshop, selects problems for improvement, selects team leaders, and guides and approves targets and measures. The process owner may function as the leader of a kaizen event or workshop, or may work with the workshop leader.

P

# process village (creating a)

The practice of grouping machines or activities by type of operation performed.

# production

The making of either a product or a service through a net-work of processes and operations.

# production preparation process (3P)

A process for designing revolutionary, breakthrough new facilities or services focused on optimizing all aspects of flow.

# productivity

The ratio of outputs (services, products, revenue, or other results) to inputs of labor or other resources.

# product–quantity analysis

A process for analyzing the relationship between different types of parts/products/services (P) and the quantity (Q) needed of each, to help line up processes for flow production.

# pull

A method for creating a system of production in which a downstream process producing to takt time signals an upstream process that the downstream process is ready for the next patient, product, or other unit of work. Pull systems control both the production of healthcare services and the movement and wait times of patients or other work between processes that cannot be combined into a production cell. *See also* kanban.

# pull system

A production system in which parts, services, and information are not produced and supplies are not replenished until exactly when they are needed, as signaled by internal and external customers. Carefully balanced schedules and buffer stocks of resources (including staffed and stocked beds and exam rooms) absorb variation in either the demand for or supply of healthcare services that otherwise might disrupt the flow. Contrast with push system.

## push system

A traditional production system in which patients, supplies, services, units or parts, and information are processed or produced at a pace that is usually unrelated to downstream readiness for more work or the master pace of patient or customer demand (takt time). The pace is sometimes dictated by a siloed production schedule, or simply set to produce as fast as possible. Processed units are pushed on to the next process regardless of whether they are needed at that time or not.

P

# Q

## quality

In healthcare, a degree of excellence that includes characteristics of appropriateness, outcomes, service, and waste: for example, Quality = appropriateness × (outcomes + service)/waste.

## quality function deployment (QFD)

A process that brings the voice of the customer into product and service development. Multi-skilled project teams use a customized house of quality matrix to define the relationships and trade-offs between patient or customer desires and product or service characteristics, and to help them reach consensus on the final product or service specifications to meet or exceed patient or customer expectations.

## queue time

*See* wait time.

## quick changeover

*See* setup reduction.

# R

## RACI

A guideline for assigning roles on a project team associated with an A3X, an A3T, or an A3P. Briefly, "R" stands for persons responsible for doing the actual work of managing the project or creating deliverables. "A" stands for the person (normally only one) who is formally accountable for the deliverables and associated outcomes. "C" stands for persons who are involved on the team as consultants, but who otherwise perform no work in creating deliverables. "I" stands for persons who will be kept informed of progress, but who otherwise perform no work in creating deliverables.

## red tag

A tag applied to items in an area targeted for improvement for which there is no specific and obvious use, including excess numbers of useable items. Tagged items are moved to temporary storage in a red-tag holding area, from which they can be redistributed to other areas that need them or disposed of after a specific time if they are not needed. Red tagging is an initial step in the 5S process improvement method.

**R**

## reliability

The probability that equipment can perform continuously without failure for a specific interval of time under stated conditions.

## reorder point

The level of inventory at which additional supplies must be ordered to ensure that items are available to meet average daily demand. When inventory drops to the reorder point, a new order is made to replenish the used items. The reorder point is instrumental in using a kanban system.

## responsible

*See* RACI.

## right-sized

A design, scheduling, or production device having a scale that allows it to be used directly within the flow of service production, so that operations no longer require unnecessary transport and waiting. Contrast with monument.

## root cause

**R**

The initiating or most fundamental cause of a problem. The root cause is often hidden by secondary or superficial causes which, when fixed, don't solve the core problem. The five why's and cause-and-effect diagrams are two simple but effective problem-solving techniques aimed at determining root cause.

# S

## safety stock

Inventory or work on hand that is held to absorb fluctuations that cannot be predicted based upon normal variation around the average. Safety stock can be determined based upon disaster planning requirements, or based upon the known failure rate of a supplying process. For disaster planning (e.g., to protect a hospital from supply chain disruptions in the event of an earthquake or flood), the amount of safety stock should be sufficient to protect production of services for the number of days anticipated to restore normal supply operations. For failures in supplying processes, safety stock should be equal to the known failure rate times the delivery lead time.

## scatter diagram

A chart in which data points are plotted to show the pattern of relationships or correlations between pairs of variables or factors. This tool is extremely useful to detect the cause of a problem, the strength of a relationship between factors, and how the change of one variable can affect another.

S

## scientific method

A rigorous method for investigation and discovery of new knowledge. Briefly, the process is as follows: (1) observe and measure some aspect of the world; (2) invent a hypothesis consistent with what has been observed; (3) use the hypothesis to make predictions; (4) test through experimentation or further observation and modify the hypothesis in light of the results; (5) repeat steps 3 and 4 until there are no discrepancies between theory and experiment and/or observation. The PDCA cycle is commonly seen as a form of the scientific method used in the context of lean and continuous improvement.

# seiketsu

The fourth of the 5S's. *See standardize.*

# seiri

The first of the 5S's. *See sort.*

# seiso

The third of the 5S's. *See shine.*

# seiton

The second of the 5S's. *See set in order.*

**S**

# sensei

A personal teacher with mastery of a body of knowledge; within Toyota, sensei–student relationships exist in many forms. In management succession, training forms around problem solving and A3 reports and the PDCA process, which are integrated into hoshin kanri. "Sensei" also refers to external consultants with deep knowledge and experience.

# servant leader

A termed coined by Robert Greenleaf in 1970 to describe a leader who "focuses primarily on the growth and well-being of people and the communities to which they belong." A servant leader in an organization shares power, puts the needs of others first, and helps people develop and perform as highly as possible. The concept aligns well with principles of lean leadership. *See also* mentor; sensei.

# service family

A set of services that tend to rely on or consume a similar constellation of resources (such as skilled clinicians, medication, equipment, and physical spaces).

# *set in order*

The second of the 5S's, to "*set in order*" (*seiton*) means to determine and systematically label standard locations for all needed items.

# setup

**S**

The tasks and associated time required whenever a physical space or machine must be reconfigured to perform a different operation or process, e.g., a linear accelerator or an operating room. There are two kinds of setup, *internal setup,* which can only be done when a machine or operation is shut down; and *external setup,* activities that can be performed while the machine or process is still operating. Also known as *changeover.*

## setup reduction

A process that focuses on reducing setup, or changeover, time; also known as *quick changeover*. The process includes reexamining operations to explore ways of converting internal setup to external setup, as well as ways to radically streamline all setup activities. The long-term objective is zero setup, in which changeovers are instantaneous and do not interfere with one-piece flow. *See also* zero changeover or zero setup.

## seven wastes

Seven types of muda, as categorized by Taiichi Ohno at Toyota:

1. Overproduction, or Excess Production—producing more, sooner, or faster than what is required by the patient or the next process.
2. Waiting—process idle time, and time delays before the next process step.
3. Transport—unnecessary or multiple handling or movement of patients, supplies, or equipment.
4. Overprocessing, or Excess Processing—unnecessary steps, work elements, or procedures.
5. Inventory, or Excess Inventory—producing, holding or purchasing unnecessary supplies or equipment.
6. Motion, or Excess Movement—unnecessary reaching, walking, or looking for patients, instruments, prints, or information; non-ergonomic motion.
7. Defects—rework and correction of errors, quality problems, and equipment problems.

## shadow board

A board or other flat surface on which the outlines or "shadows" of objects normally stored there have been painted or otherwise

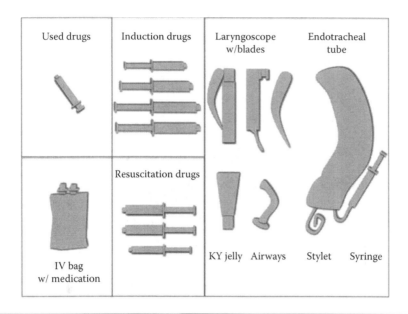

| Used drugs | Induction drugs | Laryngoscope w/blades | Endotracheal tube |
|---|---|---|---|

**Figure 9   Shadow board example for an anesthesia cart.**

attached; used to keep tools, equipment, and/or supplies in the right place and to recognize when something is missing. *See* Figure 9.

# Shewhart cycle

*See* plan-do-check-act (PDCA) cycle.

# *shine*

The third of the 5S's, *shine* (*seiso*) means to keep the first two S's in place by preventing unneeded items from accumulating, by ensuring that everything is *set in order*, and by keeping the workplace clean so that work is easier and safer to perform. In healthcare, *shine* also means to inspect for sources of contagion that may need to be addressed regularly throughout the day, not just when environmental services cleans up at the end of a shift or day.

## Shingo, Shigeo

A Japanese industrial engineer known for his skill in improving manufacturing processes. Shingo helped revolutionize the way we manufacture goods and produce services. Shingo's paramount contribution was his development in the 1960s and 1970s of poka yoke and source inspection systems, which emphasized the practical achievement of zero defects by good process engineering and investigation, as well as SMED (single minute exchange of die) techniques for setup reduction.

## shitsuke

The fifth of the 5S's. *See sustain.*

## sigma

The Greek letter $\sigma$, which stands for one standard deviation from the mean of a normal distribution. Sigma levels are a measure of process variation.

**S**

## silo

A vertically organized functional department that is self-contained (like a grain storage tower). Vertical organizations can present obstacles when it comes to seeing and improving the end-to-end process flow as experienced by patients and other customers. In lean healthcare enterprises, multidisciplinary teams work to break through the walls of these silos and consider entire value streams when designing and delivering services to patients.

## single minute exchange of die

*See* SMED.

## single-piece flow

*See* one-piece flow.

## single-point lession

*See* one-point lesson.

## six sigma

A very high level of statistical quality in which most observations fall within six sigmas, or standard deviations, from the mean of a normal distribution. At this level of quality, there are just 3.4 defects per million "products" (or opportunities for a defect to occur).

**S**

## Six Sigma

A change program originally developed at Motorola and based upon Total Quality Management, specifically focused on meeting customer requirements through reduced process variation and improved quality.

## SMED

An acronym for single-minute exchange of die, a series of operator techniques pioneered by Shigeo Shingo that result in the capability to perform machinery changeovers in less than ten minutes. The term is often used interchangeably with setup reduction (or *quick changeover*).

## SOP

*See* standard operating procedure.

## sort

The first of the 5S's, to sort (*seiso*) means to remove from the workplace all unneeded items and information and to ensure that necessary things are stored conveniently in places that correspond to the frequency of use; i.e., frequently used items should be stored close to the point of use.

## source inspection

A means of discovering errors in conditions that give rise to defects, and performing feedback and action at the error stage to prevent those errors from turning into defects.

## spaghetti chart or diagram

A map, included on a standard work sheet, that demonstrates the often circuitous and redundant path taken by a clinician, patient, or product as he, she, or it moves through an operation, process, or the healthcare value stream. Spaghetti charts help teams visualize the current physical flow and set the stage for improvement. For example, see Figure 12.

# SPC

*See* statistical process control.

# special cause variation

Variation attributable to a single cause that is not part of the process. Special cause variation can be traced, assigned to specific causes, and eliminated (or, if it is variation that is "good," implemented as part of the process). Also known as "assignable" variation.

# sponsor

*See* executive sponsor.

# stakeholder

S

A person, group, or institution having an interest in the survival and success of an organization or system. Healthcare stakeholders include patients, physicians and other clinicians, healthcare staff, hospitals and other provider organizations, insurers, businesses, and regulators, among others. The term can also refer to people who are affected by and can influence a project but who are not directly involved with doing the project work.

# standard

A rule or example that provides clear expectations. Continuous improvement methods depend on identifying and setting standards, which can then function as a baseline for improvement. Standards must be specific and scientific (based on facts or evidence), documented and communicated, and adhered to.

# standardize

The fourth of the 5S's, to standardize (*seiketsu*) means to create rules (standards) for maintaining and controlling the conditions established after implementing the three 3S's (sort, set in order, and shine), for example, by conducting regular audits and applying visual control to ensure adherence.

# standard operating procedure (SOP)

A general term for documented instructions that provide specific, detailed information about how to perform operations. The scope may be extensive, involving regulations, standards, and specifications, and take the form of manuals, change notices, and online documents and forms. *See also* standard work documentation.

**S**

# standard operations

A collective phrase referring to the set of tools, forms, methods, and definitions employed in establishing, continuously measuring, and improving standard work in an organization.

# standard task

A task performed in the same way every time, no matter who performs it. More specifically, an agreed-upon set of steps that will be employed to accomplish a particular element of work. On a standard work instruction sheet, each line records the content and time of a single standard task.

# standard time

An element of standard work that defines the timeframes associated with the production of healthcare services. These include primarily takt time, but also cycle time, wait time, and lead time.

# standard work

An agreed-upon set of work procedures that establishes the best and most reliable methods and sequences for each clinician and support staff member; also an approach that helps determine those methods and sequences. Standard work aims to maximize performance while minimizing waste in *each person's* operations and workload. The elements of standard work are (1) standard task, (2) standard work sequence, (3) standard time (takt time, cycle time, wait time, and lead time), (4) standard work in process (SWIP), and (5) standard work documentation. Once standard work has been established, it serves as the baseline for further improvement.

**S**

# standard work combination sheet

A form that uses the data recorded on the time observation form to analyze the work of individual clinicians and staff members, in particular to highlight the wastes of walking and long setups. By visually graphing the combination of manual work and walking for one operator, along with equipment processing times (or the time that a support person spends performing an additional task), the sheet can be used to help eliminate unnecessary walking and other tasks, reduce long setups, and resequence work in a more rational way so that clinicians and staff members can meet takt time. One of the five classic forms used for standard work documentation. *See* Figure 10.

# standard work documentation

The implementation of standard work is aided by the use of five classic pieces of documentation, each of which offers a different "lens" through which the work comes into focus. Usually developed in the following sequence: (1) time observation form, (2) standard work sheet, (3) percent load chart, (4) standard work combination sheet, and (5) standard work instruction sheet.

# standard work in process (SWIP)

**S**

The minimum amount of work on hand that is needed for work to progress smoothly without creating idle time or interrupting the flow of service production. In the hospital or clinic, work on hand sometimes means patients in the process; thus, SWIP can mean the standard number of patients required (no more, no less) to keep clinicians and staff members producing services and effectively treating patients at takt time. In the lab, work on hand consists of lab samples; thus, SWIP is the standard number of samples required (no more, no less) to keep lab personnel and equipment producing lab results at takt time.

rona consulting group

**Standard Work Combination Sheet**

| | | |
|---|---|---|
| Area/location: Dermatology | Operator being observed: **L. Taylor RN** | Prepared by: T. Brown<br>Date prepared: 3/8/10 |
| Process: Intake/assessment | No. required per day/shift: **30/day** | Manual: - - - - - - - - - -<br>Automatic: . . . . . . . . . . |
| Item name: **RN** | Takt time — Required: **16 min (30 pts/day)**<br>Current: **22 min (22 pts/day)** | Waiting: = = = = = = = = = =<br>Walking: ~ ~ ~ ~ ~ ~ ~ ~ ~ ~ |

| Step no. | Work description | Time: Man | Auto | Walk |
|---|---|---|---|---|
| 1 | Walk to front desk, retrieve chart/intake forms | 7" | | 10" |
| 2 | Walk to waiting area, call pt name ×2 | 4" | | 5" |
| 3 | Wait for pt to approach, greet | 5" | 30" | |
| 4 | Walk to Tx rm, set down chart/forms | | | 18" |
| 5 | Open chart/review | 8" | | |
| 6 | Interview: ask pt questions, write in chart | 3:14 | | |
| 7 | Walk to get missing form, look for form, retrieve | 8" | | 10" |
| 8 | Walk back to rm, sit, continue interview | 2:26 | | 10" |
| 9 | Walk to sink, wash hands/glove | 15" | | 3" |
| 10 | Walk to pt, Examine wound/lesions, talk to pt | 25" | | 3" |
| 11 | Walk to sink, remove gloves, wash hands | 11" | | 3" |
| 12 | Walk to desk, sit, continue interview | 38" | | 3" |
| 13 | Get up/tell pt MD will be right in | 5" | | |
| 14 | Walk out of Tx rm, shut door, flip flag | 3" | | 5" |
| 15 | Walk to find MD, talk to MD | 18" | | 13" |
| | | | | |
| | | | | |
| | | | | |
| | | | | |
| | | | | |
| | **Totals** | 8'7" | 30" | 1'23" |

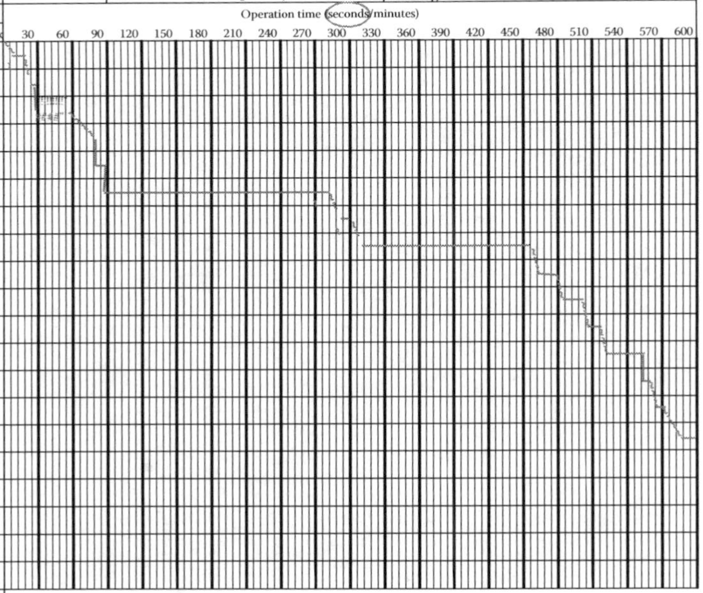


**Figure 10 Standard work combination sheet.**

S

# standard work instruction sheet

A form that details a standard work process, providing explicit instructions for new workers so that they will learn methods quickly and correctly. Each task in an operation is listed in sequence, with its description, the clinician or staff member responsible, tools and supplies required, and standard cycle

| | rona consulting group | | Operator standard work instruction |
|---|---|---|---|

| Title: Hourly rounds of support technicians | | Date: December 2010 |
|---|---|---|
| Departments who must adopt: Hospital | Operators who must adopt: Support technicians who support nurses in care of hospital patients | |

| Task # | Task description (including handoff to appropriate staff to complete task) | Task time |
|---|---|---|
| 1 | Wash hands before entering room.<br>Tools/supplies: soap, water. | 30 sec |
| 2 | Greet patient and confirm identity.<br>Tools/supplies: patient ID band, patient chart, intake forms. | 30 sec |
| 3 | Wash hands and then glove.<br>Tools/supplies: soap, water, gloves. | 30 sec |
| 4 | Toilet the patient.<br>Tools/supplies: n/a. | 150 sec |
| 5 | Deglove and wash hands.<br>Tools/supplies: soap, water. | 30 sec |
| 6 | Reposition the patient.<br>Tools/supplies: n/a. | 120 sec |
| 7 | Provide personal services as required: brush hair, clip nails, make-up, etc.<br>Tools/supplies: brush, nail clippers, etc. | 150 sec |
| 8 | Chart at bedside.<br>Tools/supplies: patient chart, pencil. | 120 sec |
| 9 | Conduct 5S activities, being careful to address potential sources of MRSA.<br>Tools/supplies: saniwipes. | 150 sec |
| 10 | | |
| 11 | | |
| 12 | | |
| **Takt time: 900 seconds/patient** | **Cycle time:** (enter observed cycle time or sum task times) | **810 sec** |

NOTE: Pictures showing the appropriate actions in sequence and by step are strongly encouraged. Attach as needed.

| Sponsor/process owner: CNO | Origin: Kaizen workshop | Version number: 2 |
|---|---|---|

© 2011 rona consulting group                                      Page 1of 1

**Figure 11    Standard work instruction sheet.**

S

time, along with supporting illustrations. One of the five classic forms used for standard work documentation. *See* Figure 11.

## standard work sequence

An agreed-upon set of steps, in an agreed-upon sequence, employed to accomplish a particular task (or cycle of work).

## standard work sheet

A form used to illustrate the process in a particular work area, including the layout of equipment, furniture, medicines, and supplies, and the movement of clinicians and other staff. Drawn during the process of time observation, it includes information on work area standards such as cycle time, work sequence, and standard work in process inventory. One of the five classic forms used for standard work documentation. *See* spaghetti diagram. *See* Figure 12.

## statistical process control (SPC)

A system of statistical techniques for quality control, based on the properties of the "bell curve" (normal statistical distribution), and used to measure and help control variation in process performance. SPC helps users separate common cause variation from special cause variation. A process is said to be "in control" when quality, as measured by the standard deviation from the mean, is equal to or greater than 99.73%.

## stop the line

The ability of any worker to stop production or services when a safety or quality problem is identified. *See also* andon cord.

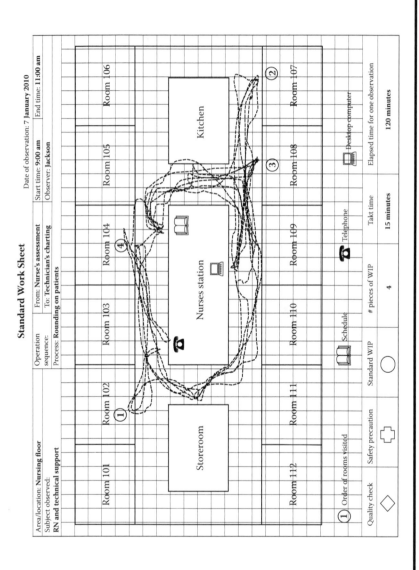

**Figure 12   Standard work sheet with spaghetti diagram.**

# storyboard

A poster-size visual representation used to exhibit the PDCA activities and key discoveries of a lean improvement team. Storyboards serve to inform, educate, and motivate other workers and teams. A3 reports are versions of storyboards.

# strategy

Generally, a careful plan or method. In the context of hoshin kanri, strategy defines a complex set of adaptive organizational activities defined by A3Ts as team-based projects that are documented on an A3X and designed to work together to achieve organizational success. *See also* hoshin.

# strategy deployment

*See* hoshin kanri.

# supermarket

Storage area for a set amount of supplies needed to provide services within the healthcare value stream. Supplies in a supermarket are withdrawn and replenished using a kanban system.

**S**

# sustain

The fifth of the 5S's, to sustain (*shitsuke*) means to continue the first four S's (sort, set in order, shine, and standardize) by making them a part of an organization's work culture and management system through ongoing visual management, communication, training, and self-discipline.

## swim-lane diagram

A cross-functional process flow chart that organizes the flow of process steps into columns or rows ("swim lanes") that represent the person or function that performs them, and illustrates the point(s) at which people or functions intersect.

## SWIP

*See* standard work in process.

**S**

# T

## takt

A German word for "time" or beat.

## takt time

The measure or rate of patient or customer demand, as calculated by time available for service production divided by average customer demand (see formula and simplified example below). Note that it is a calculated time, and is not measured with a stopwatch. For example, if a ready care clinic is open 8:00 a.m. to 8:00 p.m. with all meals and breaks staggered to provide continuous care, the available time is 12 hours, or 720 minutes; if the clinic sees 60 patients on an average day, the takt time, or rate of demand is calculated as follows:

Takt time = Available time ÷ Average demand

720 minutes available time ÷ 60 patients =

12 minute takt time

Note that this does not mean each patient encounter takes 12 minutes, but that is the rate that, on average, patients will need to move from one process to the next, and the rate at which, on average, we should see patients leaving at the end of the last process in the value stream. Takt time provides a baseline of the pace of expected daily customer demand that can be used to adjust staffing and other resource allocation decisions as actual demand fluctuates.

# task

A single discrete element of work in a larger operation or cycle of work (for example, hand washing) performed by one person (operator). *See also* standard task.

# team charter

*See* A3T.

# team leader

The person chosen to lead small group activities during a kaizen event, kaizen workshop, or other improvement activity or team. The team leader works with the workshop leader to provide input on team member selection, helps prepare for the event, facilitates the team's work on the gemba to keep things on track and support members in finding solutions, and assists with documentation and reporting.

# team member

A person who, as part of a group or team, actually performs the work of a kaizen workshop, kaizen event, or other improvement activity. There are usually 6 to 12 people on a team, including clinicians and staff members who know the process being improved; several people who are unfamiliar with the process; and sometimes a patient or customer. Team members must be able to participate for the entire duration of an improvement event.

# theory of constraints (TOC)

A theory put forth by Eliyahu Goldratt that every organization has constraints, and only by improving flow through the constraints can overall throughput be improved. He proposed an improvement process for eliminating or reducing constraints, with five steps: (1) identify the constraint; (2) decide how to exploit the constraint (how to maximize it); (3) subordinate all other resources to solving the constraint; (4) elevate the constraint (improve its capacity); and (5) if the constraint has been solved, return to step 1. For example, when delayed hospital discharges lead to poor bed availability for admissions, you first need to work on relieving the constraint by improving the discharge process so that the admissions process can be improved.

# throughput time

The time it takes for a patient, product, or service unit to proceed through a healthcare process, including both processing and wait time. Compare with lead time.

# time observation form

A form used to conduct running time studies of work, to determine the actual content of the work, and to discover opportunities for improvement. The time observation form includes the tasks performed, the actual sequence of tasks in the current state, and the actual time it takes to perform each task. One of the five classic forms used for standard work documentation. The time observation form also supports the value stream mapping process in healthcare, where it is used to document the elapsed time of a patient visit from the perspectives of the patient and the attending clinicians. *See* Figure 13.

T

rona consulting group

**Time observation form**

| Area/location: emergency department | | | | | | Date of observation: December 31, 2009 | | |
|---|---|---|---|---|---|---|---|---|
| Subject observed: patient | | | | | | Start time: 11:30 pm | | |
| Process: door to doc | | | | | | Observer: Nancy | | |

| Step no. | Description of operation | observation time | | | | | Mode (most freq. occurring) task time | Remarks |
|---|---|---|---|---|---|---|---|---|
| | | observations | | | | | | |
| | | 1 | 2 | 3 | 4 | 5 | | |
| 1 | Greet | 0 | 0:00 | 0:00 | | | 3:30 | |
| | | 3:30 | 3:00 | 4:00 | | | | |
| 2 | Wait | 3:30 | 3:00 | 4:00 | | | 5:00 | |
| | | 5:00 | 5:30 | 2:00 | | | | |
| 3 | Triage | 8:30 | 8:30 | 6:00 | | | 7:00 | 3rd patient had chest pain |
| | | 7:00 | 8:30 | 3:00 | | | | |
| 4 | Wait | 15:30 | 17:00 | 9:00 | | | 4:00 | |
| | | 5:00 | 4:00 | 1:00 | | | | |
| 5 | Register | 20:30 | 21:00 | 10:00 | | | | |

**Figure 13   Time observation form.**

# Toyota Management System

A systematic approach to managing the learning organization that combines hoshin kanri and the Toyota Production System.

# Toyota Production System (TPS)

A system and philosophy of managing production based on reducing lead time and cost and improving quality, safety, and value, through the total elimination of waste.

**T**

# total productive maintenance (TPM)

A set of methods, tools, and behaviors to ensure that every machine used in producing a service or product is always able to perform its required tasks at takt time so that production is never interrupted through the non-availability of equipment or materials, inefficiency, or defects.

## total quality management (TQM)

A systematic approach to managing quality that integrates PDCA, statistical process control, hoshin kanri, and concurrent engineering (a concept more common in manufacturing, in which cross-functional teams work together in parallel on the development of new products). Compare with Six Sigma.

## TPM

*See* total productive maintenance.

## TPS

*See* Toyota Production System.

## TQM

*See* total quality management.

T

## True North

A long-term vision for a lean enterprise; the ideal state that serves as a focal point to guide an organization's transformation.

# U

## uptime

The percentage of time a process or piece of equipment is available to produce and provide goods and services.

## U-shaped cell

A work area or cell designed in the shape of the letter "U," which is sometimes advantageous for easing tasks, shortening distances, sharing work, and facilitating communication. For example, see the cell design shown in Figure 4. *See also* cell.

U

# V

## V/A

Value added (or value adding).

## value

When a product or service is perceived by a patient or customer to fulfill a requirement, need, or desire—as defined by the patient or customer—it has value. In financial terms, value is the worth of, or the price a person is willing to pay for, a product or service such as a healthcare treatment or a medical device. Components of value include quality, usefulness, functionality, availability, price, attractiveness, and so on.

## value-added activity

An activity is said to be value-added if a patient or customer would be willing to exchange goods, services, or money for that activity. In other words, an activity adds value if it changes information about the patient, medical know-how, medicines, or supplies into a product or service that is of value for the patient. For the inpatient, it is something that improves health, learning, preparation for discharge, relief of pain, and so on. In an outpatient setting, it could be access, empathetic listening, or timely results. We would not value such things as waiting, walking, defects, overprocessing, overproduction, transportation, or inventory (in other words, waste).

V

## value-added ratio (VAR)

The percent of time in a process or value stream that the patient or customer is receiving valuable services or products. To calculate VAR for a process, divide the total value-added time in the process by the total process lead time.

Value-added ratio = Value-added time/Lead time

## value-added time

The time of those tasks or work elements in an operation or process, as recorded on the time observation form, that actually change or transform the patient's condition in a way that the patient would be willing to pay for, normally through diagnosis, pain control, and treatment.

## value stream

All the activities, operations, and processes—together with their constituent skilled people, methods, materials, medication, and equipment—required to produce a product, treatment, or service family and deliver it safely to patients or customers. *See also* clinical value stream; value stream map.

## value stream loop

A discrete subsystem of patient services, typically consisting of several processes that can be simplified and standardized, perhaps even combined and co-located to create a single production cell. *See* Figure 14.

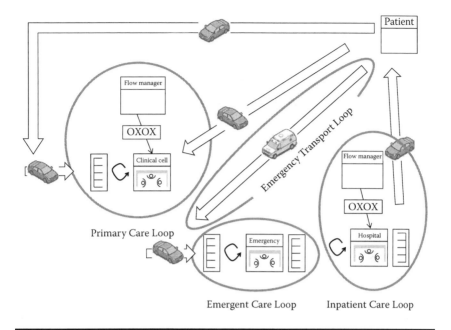

**Figure 14    Value stream loops.**

# value stream map

A diagram of a value stream that provides a way to visualize an entire flow of service production from beginning to end, so that non-value-added activities (waste) can be removed systemically rather than in isolated operations or departments. Value stream maps depict the flow of patients, materials, and information through every operation in a process, and document key information about operations, including takt time, cycle time, value-added time, non-value-added time, wait time, lead time, and value-added ratio. *See also* current state map; future state map. *See* Figures 15A and 15B.

**V**

# VAR

*See* value-added ratio.

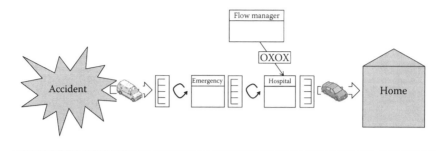

**Figure 15A  Value stream map, simplified version.**

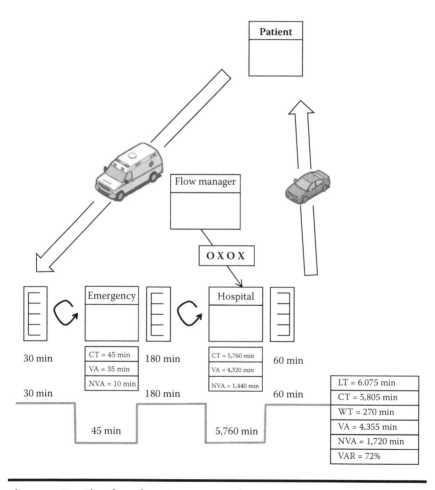

V

**Figure 15B  Simple value stream map for an acute care value stream.**

# visibility walls

Collections of documents generated through the process of hoshin kanri, including value stream maps, A3Ts, and statistics for the improvement activities chartered by the A3Ts. Visibility walls are the focal point for team review meetings, and they support leader standard work.

# visual control

A device that communicates at a glance how work should be done, including standards, procedures, the status of work in process, whether a particular process or operation is proceeding normally or abnormally, and specific countermeasures for any abnormality. *See also* andon, kanban.

# visual control system

A system of visual controls designed to create a transparent and waste-free environment in which managers, clinicians, and staff always know the current status of healthcare operations and processes, as well as the appropriate countermeasures to take when there is any abnormality.

# voice of the customer (VOC)

The desires and expectations of the patient or customer, which are of primary importance in the development of new products, services, and the daily conduct of the healthcare workplace.

**V**

# W

## wait time

The most commonly recurring elapsed time between the completion of one cycle of work (an operation or process) and the beginning of another cycle of work; for example, the time a patient spends in queue waiting for the next caregiving process to occur.

## waste

Anything that adds cost or time to the process of creating and delivering a healthcare service or product without adding value. *See also* muda; mura; muri; seven wastes.

## water spider

*See* water strider.

## water strider

A highly trained person who is capable of working in different processes as needed, or who delivers materials or even patients to, and may pick up kanban from, a production line or service area (such as a clinic exam room, hospital room, or operating room). The materials handler (or transporter, as the case may be) usually follows a specific route at specified time intervals set up to ensure that pitch integrity can be maintained throughout the value stream.

**W**

## WIP

*See* work in process.

## work in process

Patients in the process of being cared for, or information or material in the process of having value added to it. In lean enterprises, the quantity of work in process is controlled for maximum efficiency of flow. *See also* standard work in process.

## workshop leader

The highest-ranking person in a kaizen workshop, and the primary link (along with the team leader) between top management and the team.

**W**

# X

## X-matrix or X-type matrix

A type of matrix diagram designed to reveal the interactions among four sets of elements. Frequently used in hoshin kanri (policy deployment) to embody the organization's annual policy. *See also* P/O matrix; A3X.

X

# Y

## yokoten

The practice of sharing best practices and learning from improvement activities across an organization.

# Z

## zero changeover or zero setup

A setup, or changeover, procedure that can be performed in less than three minutes or within a single interval of takt time.

## zero quality control (ZQC)

A comprehensive system of quality management, aimed at producing zero defects, that incorporates self-checks and successive inspection of quality by operators and the systematic use of mistake-proofing techniques to control quality at the source. *See also* source inspection.

# HEALTHCARE
# TERMS

# A

## ABN

*See* advance beneficiary notice.

## academic medical center

An accredited, degree-granting institution of higher education, owned by a government entity or private nonprofit organization, and consisting of an allopathic or osteopathic medical school, one or more other health professions schools or programs (such as nursing, dentistry, or pharmacy), and one or more owned or affiliated teaching hospitals or health systems.

## A-CAHPS

*See* Ambulatory Care CAHPS.

## access

A patient's or consumer's ability to utilize healthcare services. Lack of access is a critical issue in healthcare, affected by the supply of healthcare providers in a geographical area, the availability and affordability of healthcare insurance, and out-of-pocket healthcare costs not covered by insurance.

## accountable care organization (ACO)

A group of healthcare providers who coordinate care and manage chronic diseases for patients, and thereby improve the quality of care. The organization's payment is tied to achieving healthcare quality goals and outcomes that result in cost savings.

## accreditation

A process through which a third-party organization evaluates a healthcare program or organization against a set of criteria and standards and recognizes institutions that meet the established standards. The accreditation process generally includes both offsite and onsite review of policies, procedures, and performance.

## ACO

*See* accountable care organization.

## ACU

*See* ambulatory care unit.

## acuity

The degree of severity or complexity of an illness. High-acuity patients generally require more care and pose higher risks.

## acute care

Services provided to treat a patient on a short-term basis for a serious episode of illness or injury that is subject to cure through medical intervention, or during recovery from surgery. Contrast with chronic care; long-term care.

## ADC

*See* average daily census.

## admission

The process through which inpatient care is initiated in a hospital, long-term care setting, or other inpatient healthcare facility. Contrast with discharge.

## admitting physician

The doctor responsible for admitting a patient to a hospital or other inpatient healthcare facility. *See also* attending physician.

## advance beneficiary notice (ABN)

A written notice that a doctor or supplier should give a Medicare beneficiary when furnishing an item or service for which Medicare is expected to deny payment. If an ABN is not provided in advance of such a service, the patient is not liable for payment.

**A**

## advance directive

A written document, recognized under law, through which a person provides instructions on how healthcare decisions will be made in the event that he or she becomes incapacitated. The two main types of advance directives are the living will and the durable power of attorney for healthcare.

## advanced practice nurse (APN) or advanced practice registered nurse (APRN)

A nurse who has earned a master's degree and can go on to work beyond the practice area of a registered nurse, as a nurse practitioner, nurse midwife, nurse anesthetist, or clinical nurse specialist.

## advanced practice provider (APP)

Refers to an advanced practitioner such as an advanced practice nurse, nurse practitioner, or physician assistant, and sometimes a licensed psychologist or licensed clinical psychologist.

## adverse event

Harm to a patient as a result of medical care, or an undesired outcome as a consequence of care such as an infection associated with use of a catheter, regardless of whether the event was preventable.

## affiliated medical staff

Medical providers that are listed on a health system or hospital's medical staff, and are normally credentialed and privileged but not employed by the hospital or system's medical group.

**A**

# Affordable Care Act

A broad U.S. healthcare reform law enacted in March, 2010 in two parts: The Patient Protection and Affordable Care Act was signed into law on March 23, 2010 and was amended by the Health Care and Education Reconciliation Act on March 30, 2010. The name "Affordable Care Act" is used to refer to the final, amended version of the law. The law is intended to expand access to health insurance, improve consumer protections, emphasize prevention and wellness, improve quality and performance, expand the health workforce, and lower healthcare costs.

# against medical advice (AMA)

Also referred to as "left against medical advice" (LAMA) or "discharge against medical advice" (DAMA), the term refers to a patient leaving a healthcare facility against the advice of his or her doctor.

# Agency for Healthcare Research and Quality (AHRQ)

An operating division of the U.S. Department of Health & Human Services (HHS) whose mission is to "produce evidence to make health care safer, higher quality, more accessible, equitable, and affordable, and to work with … HHS and other partners to make sure that the evidence is understood and used."[*]

---

[*] www.ahrq.gov

# AHRQ

*See* Agency for Healthcare Research and Quality.

# ALOS

*See* average length of stay.

# AMA

*See* against medical advice.

# ambulatory care

All types of care that do not require admission to a hospital or other healthcare institution for overnight stays. Also known as outpatient care.

# Ambulatory Care CAHPS (A-CAHPS)

A programmatic initiative within CAHPS to develop and support survey instruments that assess the quality of ambulatory care from the patient's perspective. The A-CAHPS initiative has produced the Clinician & Group Surveys as well as the updated Health Plan Surveys.* *See also* Consumer Assessment of Healthcare Providers and Systems.

# ambulatory care unit (ACU)

A healthcare facility that provides ambulatory care; typically refers to an outpatient unit of a hospital or medical center.

---

* AHRQ CAHPS Glossary

# ambulatory surgical center (ASC)

A place other than a hospital that performs outpatient surgery. Patients stay for only a few hours or for one night.

# ancillary services

Support services provided by a hospital or other inpatient health program, other than room, board, and medical and nursing professional services. These may include x-ray, drug, laboratory, or other services.

# anesthesia

Drugs administered to a patient before surgery so he or she will not feel pain. Anesthesia can be local, regional, sedative, or general. Anesthesia is an ancillary service, and is always provided by a doctor or specially trained nurse.

# APN or APRN

*See* advanced practice nurse.

# APP

*See* advanced practice provider.

# ASC

*See* ambulatory surgical center.

## attending physician

The licensed physician assigned to assume primary responsibility, legally and otherwise, for supervising all aspects of
a patient's medical care and treatment upon admission to a
hospital or other inpatient setting. Attending physicians may
also have faculty appointments and provide training to medical students, interns, and residents.

## average daily census (ADC)

The average inpatient population (excluding newborns) in
a hospital or other inpatient facility, for a given time period,
calculated as follows: Total inpatient days for a period ÷ Total
number of days in the period.

## average length of stay (ALOS)

How long, on average, patients stay as inpatients in a hospital, from the time of admission to the time of discharge.
ALOS is typically calculated as follows: Total inpatient days ÷
Total number of discharges (or total number of admissions).
Inpatient days are also referred to as *discharge days*, and are
counted to include every day in a patient stay except the day
of discharge. ALOS is an important hospital statistic used
in planning, often used as a measure of efficiency. *See also*
length of stay.

# B

## balance billing

A practice in which healthcare providers bill patients for the difference between the provider's charges for services and the amount covered or allowed by insurance.

## basic metabolic panel (BMP)

A group of blood tests that provides information about a patient's metabolism, including kidney functioning, blood acid/base balance, and blood sugar levels.

## behavioral health

A general term that encompasses the promotion of emotional health; the prevention of mental illnesses and substance use disorders; and treatments and services for substance abuse, addiction, substance use disorders, mental illness, and/or mental disorders. The term "client" is preferred to "patient" in behavioral health settings.[*]

## BMI

See body mass index.

---

[*] SAMHSA, *Leading Change: A Plan for SAMHSA's Role and Actions 2011–2014*, October 2010.

## BMP

**B**

*See* basic metabolic panel.

## board certification

A voluntary process through which physicians can become certified in a specialized area of medical practice; board certification exceeds the minimum competency required to become licensed to diagnose and treat patients, and usually requires completion of a clinical residency program as well as passing written and oral examinations.

## body mass index (BMI)

A measure of body fat based on height and weight, calculated as follows: Mass (or weight) in kilograms ÷ Height.

# C

## CAHPS

*See* Consumer Assessment of Health Providers and Systems.

## capitation

A healthcare payment system in which an insurer or other payer pays a fixed fee per patient to a healthcare provider, to cover the costs of all healthcare services for the patient for a specified length of time. Fees are set by contract between the insurer and the provider.

## care coordination

The deliberate organization of patient care activities and sharing of information among all participants in a patient's care to achieve safer and more effective care. Care coordination was identified as a top priority area for improvement in healthcare by the Institute of Medicine.

## care redesign

A process for making systematic changes to primary care practices and health systems to improve the quality, efficiency, and effectiveness of patient care, for the purpose of improving patient outcomes.[*]

---

[*] The Agency for Healthcare Research and Quality (AHRQ).

## case management

A process used by a doctor, nurse, or other health professional to manage a patient's healthcare. Case managers ensure that patients obtain needed services throughout a continuum of health and human services and care settings, track patient use of facilities and resources, and ensure that care is safe effective, patient-centered, timely, efficient, and equitable.

## case mix

The distribution of patients into categories reflecting differences in severity of illness or resource consumption.

## case mix index (CMI)

The average diagnosis-related group (DRG) relative weight for all Medicare admissions. (Each DRG has an assigned payment weight based on the average resources used for treatment.) A hospital's CMI is calculated by summing the DRG weights for all Medicare discharges and dividing by the number of discharges.

## catheter-associated urinary tract infection (CAUTI)

Urinary tract infections (UTIs), infections of any part of the urinary system, are the most commonly reported type of healthcare-associated infections. Approximately 75% of UTIs acquired by a patient during a hospital stay are associated with urinary catheters, with the most important risk factor being prolonged use of a catheter.

# CAUTI

*See* catheter-associated urinary tract infection.

# CCU

*See* coronary care unit; critical care unit.

## census

The number of inpatients present in a hospital at a particular point in time, excluding newborns.

## census days

*See* patient days.

# Center for Medicare & Medicaid Innovation (CMMI)

The Innovation Center within CMS that supports the development and testing of innovative healthcare payment and service delivery models.

# Center for Medicare/Medicaid Services (CMS)

An operating division of the U.S. Department of Health & Human Services that oversees the Medicare program, the federal portion of the Medicaid program and State Children's Health Insurance Program, the Health Insurance Marketplace, and related quality assurance activities.

## central line (CL)

A central venous catheter inserted into a large vein in a patient's neck, chest, or groin, and ending at or near the heart. Central lines are used to provide medication, nutrition, or fluids, to collect blood for medical tests, and to monitor cardio-vascular status. They are commonly used in intensive care units, can remain in place for weeks or months, and require special protocols to prevent infection.

## central line-associated bloodstream infection (CLABSI)

A laboratory-confirmed bloodstream infection where a central line had been in place for more than two calendar days and was still in place on the day of or the day before infection. CLABSIs are deadly and costly, and have been a major target for improvement.

## certified nurse practitioner (NP-C)

A nurse practitioner who has passed a national board certifying exam in his or her area of practice.

## certified registered nurse anesthetist (CRNA)

A board-certified advanced practice nurse who can perform anesthetic services for a wide range of surgical and diagnostic procedures. CRNAs can work independently or under the supervision of a physician or surgeon, depending on individual state laws.

## Checklist Manifesto

A book by surgeon and public health researcher Atul Gawande, in which he details the power of the deceptively simple checklist as a tool to prevent human error in healthcare services, including its impact on reducing CLABSIs.

**C**

# chief medical information officer (CMIO)

A healthcare executive, usually a physician, responsible for guiding the adoption and application of clinical informatics technologies in a healthcare organization, including electronic medical records, computerized physician order entry, and health information exchanges.

# chief medical officer (CMO)

A physician leader who has the chief administrative responsibility for clinical quality and who plans, organizes, and directs medical staff services for a healthcare organization.

# chief nursing officer (CNO)

A nurse leader who is the highest ranking administrative nurse in a healthcare organization, and who directs the practice of nursing and nursing standards across all clinical settings in the organization.

# chronic care management

The care of chronic disease; effectively caring for and managing chronic diseases is a key challenge of the healthcare system. Contrast with acute care.

## chronic disease

A persistent disease such as heart disease, stroke, cancer, diabetes, or arthritis. Chronic diseases are among the most common, costly, and preventable of all health problems in the U.S., and the leading causes of death and disability.

## CICU

A cardiac intensive care unit. Also called a coronary care unit (CCU).

## circulating nurse

A registered nurse who manages overall nursing care in the operating room and ensures patient safety.

## CLABSI

*See* central line-associated blood stream infection.

## CLI

*See* central line-associated blood stream infection.

## client

An alternative term for patient, used particularly in behavioral health services.

# clinical nurse specialist (CNS)

An advanced practice nurse who works in a variety of health-care settings and who has expertise in a specialized clinical area, such as pediatrics, critical care, or oncology.

# clinician

A physician, nurse practitioner, physician assistant, or other person who is qualified to practice medicine and who interacts directly with patients.

# CMI

*See* case mix index.

# CMIO

*See* chief medical information officer.

# CMO

*See* chief medical officer.

# CMS

*See* Center for Medicare/Medicaid Services.

# CNO

*See* chief nursing officer.

C

## code blue, code red

A term used in hospital settings to alert staff to an emergency situation such as a cardiac arrest (usually code blue) or a fire (usually code red), and signal them to respond.

## colonoscopy

A procedure performed by a gastroenterologist, using a long, narrow, flexible tube to examine a patient's rectum and colon in order to diagnose certain conditions and to screen for disease.

## complete blood count (CBC)

A blood test that measures the number of red and white blood cells and their size, the amount of hemoglobin, and other information about a blood sample. It is used to detect, diagnose, and monitor many health conditions.

## Consumer Assessment of Healthcare Providers and Systems (CAHPS)

A program of the U.S. Agency for Healthcare Research and Quality (AHRQ) designed to gather and report information on consumers' and patients' experiences with a variety of healthcare services. Originally known as the Consumer Assessment of Health Plans Study, CAHPS now includes a family of surveys covering health and dental plans, clinicians and groups, surgical care, behavioral health services, home healthcare, nursing homes, hospitals, and more.* *See also* A-CAHPS.

---

* For further details, see cahps.ahrq.gov.

# contract physician

A doctor who works with a hospital under contract to provide core specialty services, such as a radiologist, pathologist, anesthesiologist, or emergency room doctor.

# coordination of care

*See* care coordination.

# core measures

Clinical quality measures for hospitals.

# coronary care unit (CCU)

An intensive care unit that specializes in cardiac care.

# credentialing

The process of assessing and confirming the qualifications of a licensed or certified healthcare practitioner for inclusion on a hospital's medical staff or in a health plan.

# critical care unit (CCU)

*See* ICU.

# critical pathways

Guidelines and programs designed to reduce variation, improve quality, and reduce the costs of healthcare, particularly in high-volume hospital diagnoses, by displaying goals for patients and providing the ideal sequence and timing of staff actions for achieving those goals with optimal efficiency. Also known as critical paths, clinical pathways, or care paths.[*]

## CRNA

*See* certified registered nurse anesthetist.

## CT scan

Computed tomography scan, a type of imaging in which special x-ray equipment is used to make cross-sectional pictures of a patient's body. CT scans are used to detect broken bones, cancers, blood clots, and other health problems.

---

[*] Pearson S.D., Goulart-Fisher D., and Lee T.H. Critical pathways as a strategy for improving care: problems and potential. *Ann Intern Med.* 123 (1995):941–948.

# D

## DAMA

Discharge against medical advice. *See also* against medical advice.

## DEA registration number

A registered number assigned by the U.S. Drug Enforcement Agency to healthcare providers that allows them to prescribe controlled substances.

## decubitus ulcer

Also known as a pressure sore, an area of damaged skin caused by staying in one position too long. Decubitus ulcers can result in serious infections. Bedridden, wheelchair bound, and nursing home patients are especially at risk, and special protocols must be used for prevention.

## deeming authority

The authority granted by CMS to accrediting organizations to determine, on CMS's behalf, whether a healthcare organization is in compliance with corresponding Medicare regulations and meets CMS requirements.

# Department of Health and Human Services (HHS)

The U.S. government's principal agency for protecting the health of Americans and providing essential human services. It encompasses 11 operating divisions including, among others, the Agency for Healthcare Research and Quality (AHRQ), the Centers for Disease Control and Prevention (CDC), the Centers for Medicare and Medicaid Services (CMS), the Food and Drug Administration (FDA), the National Institutes of Health (NIH), and the Substance Abuse and Mental Health Services Administration (SAMHSA).

# diagnosis-related group (DRG)

A classification system that groups patients according to diagnosis, type of treatment, age, and other relevant criteria. The system is used by CMS to reimburse hospitals based on a patient's diagnosis. Under the prospective payment system, hospitals are paid a set fee for treating patients in a single DRG category, regardless of the actual cost of care for the individual.

# discharge days

*See* inpatient days.

# discharge planning

A complex and critical healthcare process used to decide what a patient needs for a smooth move from one level of care to another, including moves from a hospital to a nursing home or home care. Planning is done by a social worker, case manager, or other healthcare professional, sometimes involving the services of home health agencies, but the actual hospital discharge must be authorized by a physician.

**D**

## DME

*See* durable medical equipment.

## DNR

*See* do not resuscitate (DNR) order.

## do not resuscitate (DNR) order

A medical order written by a doctor after consultation with a patient or a patient's healthcare proxy or family, instructing healthcare providers not to do cardiopulmonary resuscitation (CPR) if breathing stops or if the heart stops beating. A DNR order allows a patient to choose before an emergency occurs whether he or she wants CPR; it does not affect other treatments, such as medication or nutrition.

## DRG

*See* diagnosis-related group.

## durable medical equipment (DME)

Purchased or rented items covered by Medicare, such as hospital beds, iron lungs, oxygen equipment, seat lift equipment, wheelchairs, and other medically necessary and reusable equipment prescribed by a healthcare provider to be used in a patient's home.

## D    durable power of attorney

A legal document that enables you to designate another person, called the attorney-in-fact, to act on your behalf, in the event you become disabled or incapacitated.

# E

## ED

*See* emergency department/emergency room.

## EHR

*See* electronic health record.

## electronic health record (EHR)

A digital version of a patient's paper medical chart that contains information from all clinicians involved in a patient's care and can be easily shared among providers in different healthcare organizations including laboratories, specialists, and pharmacies. EHRs also allow access to evidence-based tools providers can use to make care decisions and automate and streamline provider workflow. Contrast with electronic medical record.

## electronic medical record (EMR)

A digital version of a patient's paper medical chart that contains a patient's medical history from one provider's practice, used mainly for diagnosis and treatment, and not easily shared with other providers. It allows providers to track data over time, identify patients who are due for care, monitor patients, and improve overall quality of care. Contrast with electronic health record.

## emergency department (ED)/ emergency room (ER)

A hospital area or department or free-standing medical unit appropriately equipped and staffed to diagnose and treat unforeseen illness or trauma expeditiously.

**E**

## Emergency Medical Treatment and Active Labor Act (EMTALA)

An act of U.S. Congress requiring any Medicare-participating hospital that operates a hospital emergency department to provide an appropriate medical screening examination to any patient that requests it, regardless of ability to pay, national origin, race, creed, or color. If the hospital determines that the patient has an emergency medical condition, it must either stabilize the patient's condition or arrange for a transfer; however, the hospital may only transfer the patient if the medical benefits of the transfer outweigh the risks or if the patient requests the transfer.

## EMR

*See* electronic medical record.

## EMTALA

*See* Emergency Medical Treatment and Active Labor Act.

## EOB

*See* explanation of benefits.

# ePHI

*See* protected health information.

# ER

*See* emergency department/emergency room.

E

# ESRD

End-stage renal disease, or permanent kidney failure with dialysis or a transplant.

# evidence-based medicine or practice

Applying the best available research results (evidence) when making decisions about healthcare. Healthcare professionals who perform evidence-based practice use research evidence along with clinical expertise and patient preferences. Systematic reviews (summaries of healthcare research results) provide information that aids in the process of evidence-based practice.

# explanation of benefits (EOB)

A form provided by insurance companies to covered individuals and to healthcare providers, detailing the amounts of medical claims, benefits allowed, amounts paid, patient balances, and amounts denied, with explanations for denials or adjustments.

# F

## fasting blood sugar (FBS)

A measurement of blood glucose level after not eating or drinking for eight hours, used to detect diabetes.

## FBS

*See* fasting blood sugar.

## fee for service (FFS)

A healthcare payment system in which an insurer or other payer pays healthcare providers for services rendered. Contrast with capitation.

## FFS

*See* fee for service.

## for-profit hospital/health system

An investor-owned hospital or multihospital corporation that operates under the same rules and regulations as a not-for-profit hospital, but a key purpose is to return a profit to investors. Most for-profits are not tax exempt.

# G

## gastrointestinal (GI) endoscopy

A procedure that uses a lighted, flexible endoscope to see inside the upper GI tract, including the esophagus, stomach, and duodenum—the first part of the small intestine. It is used to detect GI disorders, diagnose illnesses, and perform biopsies.

## GI

Gastrointestinal.

# H

## HCAHPS

*See* Hospital Consumer Assessment of Healthcare Providers and Systems.

## HCC

*See* hierarchical condition category model.

## healthcare (or health care)

The maintaining and restoration of physical and mental health by the treatment and prevention of disease, illness, and injury, performed by healthcare providers.

## Healthcare Effectiveness Data and Information Set (HEDIS®)

A tool developed and maintained by the National Committee for Quality Assurance (NCQA) and used by U.S. health plans to assess performance on 75 measures of care and service across 8 domains. HEDIS allows consumers to compare performance across health plans.*

---

\* NCQA.

# health information exchange (HIE)

An electronic information exchange that allows doctors, nurses, pharmacists, other healthcare providers, and patients to appropriately access and securely share a patient's vital medical information electronically—improving the speed, quality, safety, and cost of patient care.

# Health Insurance Portability and Accountability Act (HIPAA)

A Federal law that allows persons to qualify immediately for comparable health insurance coverage when they change employers. It also gives HHS the authority to mandate the use of standards for the electronic exchange of healthcare data; to specify what medical and administrative code sets should be used within those standards; to require the use of national identification systems for healthcare patients, providers, payers (or plans), and employers (or sponsors); and to specify the types of measures required to protect the security and privacy of personally identifiable healthcare information. The major impact of HIPAA on lean initiatives is the section on security and privacy matters, which influences the tracking of patient identity through visual management. Also known as the Kennedy-Kassebaum Bill, the Kassebaum-Kennedy Bill, K2, or Public Law 104-191.

# health maintenance organization (HMO)

A type of health insurance plan or system that usually limits coverage to care from doctors who work for or contract with the HMO. It generally won't cover out-of-network care except in an emergency. An HMO may require enrollees to live or work in its service area to be eligible for coverage. HMOs often provide integrated care and focus on prevention and wellness, and typically offer coverage with minimal out-of-pocket costs to enrollees.

## HEDIS®

*See* Healthcare Effectiveness Data and Information Set.

**H**

## HHA

*See* home health agency.

## HHS

*See* Department of Health and Human Services.

## hierarchical condition category (HCC) model

A risk adjustment model implemented by CMS to adjust capitation payments to private healthcare plans for the health expenditure risk of their enrollees. The model centers on the use of 70 condition categories that more accurately predict risk than the previous demographic models used.

## HIPAA

*See* Health Insurance Portability and Accountability Act.

## home health agency (HHA)

An organization that gives home care services, such as skilled nursing care, physical therapy, occupational therapy, speech therapy, and personal care by home health aides.

## hospice care

End-of-life care, including medical, psychological, and spiritual support for the dying and services to support the patient's family. Hospice care can be provided at home, in a hospice center, in a hospital, or in a skilled nursing facility.

## Hospital Consumer Assessment of Healthcare Providers and Systems (HCAHPS)

Also known as Hospital CAHPS, HCAHPS is a national, standardized, publicly reported survey instrument and data collection methodology for measuring patients' perceptions of their hospital experience, that allows valid comparisons to be made across hospitals locally, regionally, and nationally. *See also* Consumer Assessment of Healthcare Providers and Systems (CAHPS).

## hospitalist

A physician who works as a full-time, salaried employee of a hospital assigned to care for inpatients on a given shift.

## Hospital Value-Based Purchasing Program (VBP)

A CMS initiative that rewards acute-care hospitals with incentive payments for the quality of care they provide to people with Medicare. Hospitals are rewarded based on how closely they follow best clinical practices and how well they enhance patients' experiences of care.

## hourly rounding

The nursing practice of checking on patients hourly, or at regular intervals, to help prevent falls and pressure ulcers, and to improve safety, quality of care, and patient satisfaction.

H

# I

## ICD-9

The ninth revision of the *International Classification of Diseases*, covering years 1979–1998.

## ICD-10

The tenth revision of the *International Classification of Diseases*, covering years 1999–present.

## ICU

*See* intensive care unit.

## IDS

*See* integrated delivery system.

## IHI

*See* Institute for Healthcare Improvement.

## IM injection

*See* intramuscular injection.

## independent physician association (IPA)

A group of independent physicians organized as a legal entity to contract with insurance companies, managed care organizations, or HMOs to provide services according to an agreed-upon fee structure.

## infusion center

An ambulatory center in which patients can receive infusion therapy—the administration of drugs through an intravenous line, a catheter, or an injection—without requiring hospitalization.

## inpatient care

The care of patients that have been admitted to a hospital or other healthcare facility.

## inpatient days

The total number of days in a patient stay in a hospital or other healthcare facility, excluding the day of discharge; also called *discharge days*. *See also* length of stay; average length of stay.

## Institute for Healthcare Improvement (IHI)

An independent, not-for-profit organization founded in the 1980s by Dr. Donald Berwick with the purpose of improving the healthcare system.

# integrated delivery system (IDS)

An organized, coordinated, and collaborative network that links various healthcare providers to provide a coordinated, vertical continuum of services to a particular patient population or community. An IDS is accountable, both clinically and fiscally, for the clinical outcomes and health status of the population or community served, and has systems in place to manage and improve them.*

# integrated medical record

*See* electronic health record; electronic medical record.

# intensive care unit (ICU)

A critical care unit of a hospital in which seriously ill patients receive specialized and concentrated care from doctors called intensivists and other specially trained staff who have access to advanced medical equipment.

# intensivist

A hospitalist who specializes in intensive care.

---

* Enthoven, A.C. Integrated delivery systems: The cure for fragmentation. *Am J Manag Care* 15, 10 Suppl (2009):S284–290.

# intern

A medical student in the first year of clinical training following medical school.

# International Classification of Diseases (ICD)

A standard diagnostic tool, developed and periodically revised by the World Health Organization (WHO) for epidemiology, health management, and clinical purposes. The ICD is used to classify and code diseases and other health problems on many types of health records, including mortality and morbidity data on death certificates. The codes are also used for reimbursement and decision-making purposes. *See also* ICD-9; ICD-10.

# intramuscular (IM) injection

An injection of medication directly into a muscle.

# intravenous line (IV)

A needle or tube inserted into a vein, used to provide patients with medications or fluids.

# intubation

A procedure used in emergency rooms and during surgery, in which an airway is established in a patient by inserting a tube through the mouth or nose into the trachea or windpipe.

# in vitro

Latin for "in glass," *in vitro* refers to tests, experiments, or procedures performed outside a living organism, for instance in a test tube or other container.

# in vivo

Latin for "in the living," *in vivo* refers to tests, experiments, or procedures performed on or in a living organism, for instance when drugs are tested on animals or in clinical trials.

# IPA

*See* independent physician association.

# IV

*See* intravenous line.

# J

## Joint Commission, The

An independent, not-for-profit organization that accredits and certifies more than 20,000 healthcare organizations and programs in the U.S.

J

# L

## LAMA

Left against medical advice. *See also* against medical advice.

## LCP

*See* licensed clinical psychologist.

## Leapfrog Group

An initiative driven by organizations that buy healthcare and are working to initiate breakthrough improvements in the safety, quality, and affordability of healthcare in the U.S. Specific Leapfrog initiatives include the Leapfrog Hospital Survey, the Hospital Safety Score, Leapfrog Hospital Recognition Program, and the Hidden Surcharge Calculator.

## length of stay (LOS)

The duration of a single hospitalization for an individual patient, calculated by subtracting the date of admission from the date of discharge, with same-day admission and discharge counting as one day. *See also* inpatient days; average length of stay.

## licensed clinical psychologist (LCP)

A state-licensed health service professional who provides professional services relating to the diagnosis, assessment, evaluation, treatment, and prevention of psychological, emotional, psychophysiological, and behavioral disorders in individuals across the lifespan.

## licensed practical nurse (LPN)

A nurse who has completed a 12- to 14-month training program, passed a licensing exam, and provides basic patient care in hospitals, nursing homes, and physician offices, usually under the supervision of an RN, APRN, or physician.

## licensed psychologist (LP)

*See* licensed clinical psychologist.

**L**

## licensed vocational nurse (LVN)

*See* licensed practical nurse.

## licensure

The granting of a license to practice as a healthcare professional (doctor, nurse, pharmacist, etc.), or to operate a healthcare facility such as a hospital or nursing home. Licenses are generally granted by state government agencies.

## long-term care

Services that help people with health or personal needs and activities of daily living over a period of time. Long-term care can be provided at home, in the community, or in various types of facilities, including nursing homes and assisted living facilities.

## LOS

*See* length of stay.

## LP

*See* licensed psychologist.

## LPN

*See* licensed practical nurse.

## LVN

Licensed vocational nurse. *See* licensed practical nurse.

# M

## magnetic resonance imaging (MRI)

A medical imaging technique that uses a large magnet and radio waves to look at a patient's organs and structures. MRI scans are used to diagnose a variety of conditions, and are very useful for examining the brain and spinal cord.

## managed care organization or system

An organization that integrates the financing and delivery of appropriate healthcare services to covered individuals by means of arrangements with selected providers to furnish a comprehensive set of healthcare services to members, explicit criteria for the selection of healthcare providers, and significant financial incentives for members to use providers and procedures associated with the plan. Managed care plans typically are labeled as HMOs (staff, group, IPA, and mixed models), PPOs, or Point of Service plans. Managed care services are reimbursed using a variety of methods including capitation, fee for service, and a combination of the two.

## Medicaid

A joint U.S. federal and state program that helps with medical costs for some people with low incomes and limited resources. Medicaid programs vary from state to state, but most healthcare costs are covered if a patient qualifies for both Medicare and Medicaid.

## medical assistant

A clinical and administrative assistant who generally works in an ambulatory setting such as a doctor's office, and who may perform a variety of tasks, from greeting patients and updating medical records to taking blood pressures and collecting laboratory specimens. Medical assistants usually receive a certificate through post-secondary education.

## medical center

A hospital facility that generally provides a complex array of healthcare services; *see also* academic medical center.

## Medical Emergency Team

**M**

*See* Rapid Response Team.

## medical home

A model for primary care, developed to improve quality of care, safety, and chronic care management to reduce costs, in which a team of primary care providers and sometimes specialists coordinate comprehensive care for patients across all areas of the healthcare system. Also known as the patient-centered medical home.

## medically necessary

Services or supplies that are proper and needed for the diagnosis or treatment of a patient's medical condition; meet the standards of good medical practice in the local area; and are not mainly for the convenience of a patient or doctor.

# Medicare

The U.S. federal health insurance program for people 65 years of age or older, certain younger people with disabilities, and people with end-stage renal disease (permanent kidney failure with dialysis or a transplant, sometimes called ESRD).

# methicillin-resistant staphylococcus aureus (MRSA)

A bacteria that is resistant to many antibiotics. In the community, most MRSA infections are skin infections. In medical facilities, MRSA causes life-threatening bloodstream infections, pneumonia, and surgical site infections.

# morbidity

**M**

Incidence and severity of illness and accidents in a well-defined class or classes of individuals.

# mortality

Incidence of death in a well-defined class or classes of individuals.

# MRI

*See* magnetic resonance imaging.

# MRSA

*See* methicillin-resistant staphylococcus aureus.

# N

## National Committee for Quality Assurance (NCQA)

A private, not-for-profit organization dedicated to improving healthcare quality; developer of the HEDIS performance measurement system.

## National Patient Safety Foundation (NPSF)

An independent, not-for-profit organization that partners with patients and families, the healthcare community, and key stakeholders to advance patient safety and healthcare workforce safety and disseminate strategies to prevent harm.

## National Quality Forum (NQF)

A nonprofit, nonpartisan, public service organization working to transform the U.S healthcare system, notably through the review, endorsement, and recommendation of standardized healthcare performance measures.

## NCQA

*See* National Committee for Quality Assurance.

## near miss

A medical error that is detected and corrected before it affects the patient.

## negative

A normal test; a test that fails to show a positive result.

## NICU

A neonatal intensive care unit, which specializes in the care of premature infants and other newborns with special medical needs.

## nosocomial infection

An infection acquired in a hospital.

## not-for-profit hospital/health system

Hospitals or healthcare systems that operate on the principle that no net revenue or profit is paid to individuals or organizations based on investment in, or ownership of, the nonprofit organization. Any profits are retained and reinvested in the organization. Most not-for-profits are tax-exempt.

## NP

*See* nurse practitioner.

# NP-C

*See* certified nurse practitioner.

# NPSF

*See* National Patient Safety Foundation.

# NQF

*See* National Quality Forum.

# NRC Picker

A leading family of surveys on the performance of healthcare providers based on the patient and family experience in a variety of settings. The surveys were originally developed by the Picker Institute, which was acquired by the National Research Corporation (NRC) in 2001.

# nurse practitioner (NP)

An advanced practice nurse who can provide a broad range of healthcare services. NPs work in a variety of settings, either independently or in a team with doctors. They perform physical exams; order tests; diagnose, treat, and manage diseases and injuries; write prescriptions; and perform procedures. State laws determine their authority and scope of practice.

# O

## Obamacare

*See* Affordable Care Act.

## observation care or observation status

A well-defined set of specific, clinically appropriate services, which include ongoing short-term treatment, assessment, and reassessment before a decision can be made regarding whether a patient will be admitted as a hospital inpatient or discharged. Observation services are commonly ordered for patients who present to the emergency department and who then require a significant period of treatment or monitoring in order to make a decision concerning their admission or discharge. Observation services are covered by Medicare only when provided by the order of a physician or another individual authorized by state licensure law and hospital staff bylaws to admit patients to the hospital or to order outpatient tests. Because observation care is classified as outpatient care, it can affect the benefits Medicare will pay for any subsequent skilled nursing care that is required.

## oncology

A branch of medicine dealing with cancer.

## outcomes/outcomes measurement

A clinical outcome is a health state of a patient resulting from healthcare. Outcome measurement depends on data about health states of patients. Outcome measurement is essential to assessing quality of care.[*]

## outpatient care

*See* ambulatory care.

O

---

[*] National Quality Measures Clearinghouse of the Agency for Healthcare and Quality, www.qualitymeasures.ahrq.gov.

# P

## PA, PA-C

*See* physician assistant.

## PACU

*See* post-anesthesia care unit.

## palliative care

Care that improves the comfort and quality of the life of a patient, including treatment of the discomfort, symptoms, and stress of serious illness such as pain, loss of appetite, and sleep problems. Hospice care always includes palliative care, but patients may receive palliative care at any stage of an illness.

P

## patient assessment

A systematic process for collecting information about a patient's overall health status, including physical and psychosocial factors, performed by a nurse or other medical professional. The process generally includes patient interview, physical examination, and sometimes diagnostic clinical testing such as blood tests or x-rays.

## patient-centered care

A model of care in which patients participate actively in their care, and treatment plans encompass patient preferences. Contrasts with a disease-centered model in which a healthcare provider's clinical experience and test data drive almost all treatment decisions.

## patient-centered medical home (PCMH)

*See* medical home.

## patient days (census days)

The number of days that inpatients (excluding newborns in the nursery) are hospitalized; a cumulative census for a time period, necessary for calculating average length of stay and occupancy rates. The day of admission, but not the day of discharge, is counted as a patient day. If both admission and discharge occur the same day, the day is counted as one patient day.

**P**

## patient experience

The patient's experience of care provided including patient satisfaction and quality of care. Patient experience is a key determinant of quality of care. It is an important element of the HCAHPS survey; results are published, allowing consumers to compare hospital scores. It is also a key component of the Hospital Value-Based Purchasing Program (VBP), which affects how Medicare reimburses hospitals for services rendered.

# patient safety alert

A system through which staff can halt healthcare activities whenever the potential for harm to a patient is detected, so that corrective actions can be initiated.

# patient satisfaction

*See* patient experience.

# payer or payor

A party other than the patient with payment responsibility for healthcare services, for instance, an insurance company or health-plan sponsor such as an employer.

# pay for performance

A reimbursement system in which providers are compensated by payers for meeting certain pre-established measures for quality and efficiency. Pay-for-performance programs have been implemented by both Medicare and private insurers, and CMS has numerous pilot projects underway in a range of clinical settings.

**P**

# PCMH

Patient-centered medical home.

# perinatal care

Maternity and neonatal care.

## perioperative

Relating to surgery and the time span around a surgical operation, usually including pre-op, surgery, and post-anesthesia care.

## peripherally inserted central catheter (PICC line)

A type of central line inserted into the arm for prolonged use, for instance, in chemotherapy or long-term antibiotic therapy.

## personal health information (PHI)

*See* protected health information.

## personal health record (PHR)

A patient-maintained electronic medical record.

## PHI

*See* protected health information.

## PHR

*See* personal health record.

## physician assistant (PA, PA-C)

A clinician who is certified and state-licensed to practice medicine with a substantial level of independence but under the supervision of a licensed physician. PAs are formally trained to provide diagnostic, therapeutic, and preventive healthcare services, can perform procedures, and make rounds in hospitals and nursing homes.

## physician extender

A skilled healthcare professional, such as a physician assistant (PA) or nurse practitioner (NP), a certified registered nurse anesthetist (CRNA), or a clinical nurse specialist (CNS) with an advanced degree that allows them to assist physicians in caring for patients.

## physician hospital organization (PHO)

A type of integrated delivery system that links hospitals and a group of physicians for the purpose of contracting directly with employers and managed care organizations. A PHO is a legal entity that allows physicians to continue to own their practices and to see patients under the terms of a professional services agreement. This type of arrangement offers the opportunity to better market the services of both physicians and hospitals as a unified response to managed care.

**P**

## PICC line

*See* peripherally inserted central catheter.

## PICU

A pediatric intensive care unit.

# point-of-service plan (POS)

A type of insurance plan in which patients incur lower co-pays and deductibles when they use doctors, hospitals, and other healthcare providers that belong to the plan's network. They can also see non-network providers, subject to higher co-pays and deductibles. POS plans require a referral from a patient's primary care doctor in order to see a specialist.

# population management

A new business model centered on delivery of comprehensive care and management of total cost risk. Organizations on the transition path to population health management must prioritize three foundational elements: (1) information-powered clinical decision making, (2) a primary care–led clinical workforce, and (3) patient engagement and community integration.*

# POS

**P**

*See* point-of-service plan.

# positive

An abnormal test result.

# post-anesthesia care unit (PACU)

A unit in a hospital or ambulatory care center designed for patients recovering from anesthesia; usually near a surgical area or operating room.

---

* "Three Key Elements for Successful Population Health Management," Advisory Board Company.

## post-op

Post-operative; the period following surgery.

## PPO

*See* preferred provider organization.

## PPS

*See* prospective payment system.

## practice guidelines

Evidence-based recommendations on current best clinical practices for diagnosis, testing, procedures, and treatments.

**P**

## pre-existing condition

A health problem a patient had before the date that a new insurance policy starts.

## preferred provider organization (PPO)

A type of health plan that contracts with medical providers, such as hospitals and doctors, to create a network of participating providers. Patients pay less if they use providers that belong to the plan's network. Patients can use doctors, hospitals, and providers outside of the network for an additional cost.

## pre-registration

A process used by a healthcare facility prior to an outpatient procedure or planned inpatient admission in order to verify a patient's demographic, insurance, and other pertinent information in advance of a scheduled patient visit.

## Press Ganey

A leading provider of patient satisfaction surveys used to rate healthcare providers, and sometimes to determine their compensation.

## pressure sore or ulcer

*See* decubitus ulcer.

## primary care

Health services that cover a range of prevention, wellness, and treatment for common illnesses. Primary care providers include doctors, nurses, nurse practitioners, and physician assistants. They often maintain long-term relationships with patients and treat a range of health-related issues. They may also coordinate care with specialists.

## prior authorization

Approval required from a health plan or insurer before a healthcare service is performed or a prescription filled, in order for the service to be covered.

# prospective payment system (PPS)

Also called prospective pricing; a payment method in which the payment a hospital will receive for patient treatment is set up in advance; hospitals keep the difference if they incur costs that are less than the fixed price in treating the patient, and they absorb any loss if their costs exceed the fixed price. *See also* diagnosis-related group.

# protected health information (PHI)

Under the HIPAA Privacy Rule, individually identifiable health information that can be linked to a particular person. Specifically, this information can relate to an individual's past, present, or future physical or mental health or condition; provision of healthcare to the individual; or past, present, or future payment for the provision of healthcare to the individual. Common identifiers of health information include names, social security numbers, addresses, and birth dates. The HIPAA Security Rule applies to individually identifiable health information in electronic form or electronic protected health information (ePHI). It is intended to protect the confidentiality, integrity, and availability of ePHI when it is stored, maintained, or transmitted.

**P**

# provider

A term used to identify an individual or organization who provides and receives payment for medical care or health services (for example, a physician, physician assistant, nurse practitioner, hospital, or nursing care facility).

# public health

A field that seeks to improve lives and the health of communities through the prevention and treatment of disease and the promotion of healthy behaviors such as healthy eating and exercise.

P

# Q

## quaternary care

Extremely specialized and advanced care including experimental medicine, provided in a limited number of healthcare facilities.

# R

## Rapid Response Team

A team of clinicians that brings critical care expertise to a patient when and where needed.

## readmission

Admission to a hospital within a certain time of being discharged from the same or another hospital. The benchmark timeframe set for tracking readmissions by CMS is 30 days. CMS penalizes hospitals for excess readmissions by reducing their reimbursement.

## registered nurse (RN)

A nursing school graduate who has been licensed to provide patient care. RNs work in a variety of settings including ambulatory facilities, hospitals, emergency rooms, physician offices, and skilled nursing facilities.

**R**

## reportable event

*See* serious reportable event.

## resident

A medical student in post-graduate clinical training following medical school.

# risk adjustment

A statistical process that takes into account the underlying health status and health spending of the enrollees in an insurance plan when looking at their healthcare outcomes or healthcare costs.

# risk pool

Arrangement by a state to provide health insurance to the unhealthy uninsured who have been rejected for coverage by insurance carriers.

# RN

*See* registered nurse.

# room turnover

The time it takes between patients to clean and prepare a hospital room, operating room, examination room, or other area in which care is provided.

**R**

# RTC

Abbreviation for "return to clinic," often used on medical charts to indicate the date on which a patient is next scheduled to be seen.

# S

## safety net hospital

A hospital that has an "open door" policy to all individuals regardless of their ability to pay. This policy can derive from either a legal mandate to care for charity patients or a mission-driven commitment to such patients.

## scrub tech

A surgical technologist, or operating room technician, who prepares operating rooms, arranges equipment, and assists doctors during surgeries.

## secondary care

Care provided by a medical specialist or facility, usually upon referral by a primary care provider.

## sentinel event

As defined by The Joint Commission, an unexpected occurrence involving death or serious physical or psychological injury, or the risk thereof. Such events are called *sentinel* because they signal the need for immediate investigation and response.

## sepsis

An illness in which the body has a severe immune response to bacteria or other germs; also called systemic inflammatory response syndrome (SIRS).

S

## serious reportable event (SRE) or incident (SRI)

A serious adverse event required to be reported to state and/or federal government agencies. As developed by the National Quality Forum for HHS, any one of a specific list of events in healthcare that are considered to be unambiguous, largely preventable, serious, and either adverse, indicative of a problem in a healthcare setting's safety systems, and/or important for public credibility or accountability. SREs include both injuries occurring during care management and errors occurring from failure to follow standard care or institutional policies and procedures.

## service family

A set of healthcare services that tend to consume a similar constellation of resources: skilled clinicians, medication, equipment, physical spaces, etc.

## service line

Healthcare organizations often organize their clinical processes into organizational divisions known as "service lines" across inpatient and ambulatory lines; for example, primary care, specialty services, surgical services, inpatient services, administrative services.

**S**

## skilled nursing care

A level of care that includes services that can only be performed safely and correctly by a licensed nurse (either a registered nurse or a licensed practical nurse).

# skilled nursing facility

A facility that meets specific regulatory certification requirements and primarily provides inpatient skilled nursing care
and related services to patients who require medical, nursing,
or rehabilitative services, but does not provide the level of
care or treatment available in a hospital.

# SNF

*See* skilled nursing facility.

# SRE or SRI

*See* serious reportable event.

# staff physician

An independently practicing physician who has been
approved as a member of a hospital's medical staff, and who
therefore has access to hospital facilities for patient admissions,
tests, and procedures. *See also* attending physician.

**S**

# subacute care

Generally, a level of care greater than that provided in a
skilled nursing facility but that does not meet the criteria for
hospital acute care.

# T

## TCAB

*See* Transforming Care at the Bedside.

## tertiary care

Specialized consultative healthcare provided upon referral from a primary care or secondary care provider, usually for inpatients, for complex health services such as cancer management or for neurosurgery.

## third-party administrator (TPA)

An entity required to make, or responsible for making, payment on behalf of a group health plan, and that handles administrative functions such as claims processing.

## TPA

*See* third-party administrator.

## transfer

Movement of patients between inpatient units or care settings, based on acuity.

## Transforming Care at the Bedside (TCAB)

An initiative through which IHI and the Robert Wood Johnson Foundation created a framework for change on medical-surgical units built around safe reliable care, teamwork, patient-centered care, and value-added care processes.

## triage

A process for evaluating patients to determine the degree of urgency of illnesses or injuries in order to prioritize patients for further diagnosis and treatment.

## Triple Aim

A framework developed by the Institute for Healthcare Improvement that describes an approach to optimizing health system performance in three dimensions: improving the patient experience of care (including quality and satisfaction), improving the health of populations, and reducing the per capita cost of healthcare.

**T**

# U

## urgent care

Care for an illness, injury, or condition serious enough that a reasonable person would seek care right away, but not so severe as to require emergency room care. Urgent care centers are ambulatory healthcare facilities that provide walk-in, extended-hour access for acute illness and injury care.

## UTI

Urinary tract infection.

## utilization

The measure of a population's use of various healthcare services available to them, including use of hospitals, physicians, and other providers. Used to examine how efficiently a healthcare system produces health in a population.

**U**

# V

## value-based purchasing

Linking provider payments to improved performance by healthcare providers. This form of payment holds healthcare providers accountable for both the cost and quality of care they provide. It attempts to reduce inappropriate care and to identify and reward the best-performing providers.

## VAP

*See* ventilator-associated pneumonia.

## VBP

*See* value-based purchasing; Hospital Value-Based Purchasing Program.

## ventilator

A device that assists or controls respiration continuously through a tracheostomy or by endotracheal intubation.

## ventilator-associated pneumonia (VAP)

A pneumonia where the patient is on mechanical ventilation for more than two calendar days on the date of the event, and the ventilator was in place on the date of event or the day before.

# W

## WHO surgical safety checklist

A tool developed as an initiative of the World Health Organization (WHO) that helps surgical teams eliminate surgical errors for all tasks required during three phases of surgery.

W

# Appendix: Sources Consulted

In addition to information derived from the Rona Consulting Group team's expertise, the following sources were used to compile and verify the material in this volume.

# Lean Terms

## *Principal References*

Productivity Press and the Productivity Group, Mary A. Junewick, ed. *LeanSpeak: The Productivity Business Improvement Dictionary* (New York: Productivity Press, 2002).

Rona Consulting Group blog, http://www.ronaconsulting.com/blog

Rona Consulting Group & Productivity Press, Thomas L. Jackson, ed. Lean Tools for Healthcare Series (New York: Productivity Press).
*5S for Healthcare*, 2009.
*Kaizen Workshops for Lean Healthcare*, 2013.
*Mapping Clinical Value Streams*, by Thomas L. Jackson, 2013.
*Mistake Proofing for Lean Healthcare*, forthcoming.
*Standard Work for Lean Healthcare*, 2012.

## *Additional References*

Camp, Robert. *Benchmarking: The Search for Industry Best Practices That Lead to Superior Performance* (New York: Productivity Press, 2006).

Jackson, Thomas L., with Karen R. Jones. *Implementing a Lean Management System* (Portland, OR: Productivity Press, 1996).

Mann, David. *Creating a Lean Culture: Tools to Sustain Lean Conversions*, 2nd edition (New York: Productivity Press, 2010).

Shingo, Shigeo. *Zero Quality Control: Source Inspection and the Poka-Yoke System* (Cambridge, MA: Productivity Press, 1986).

# Healthcare Terms

## *Principal References*

Centers for Disease Control and Prevention (CDC). http://www.cdc.gov

Centers for Medicare and Medicaid Services (CMS), Glossary. http://www.cms.gov/apps/glossary/

HealthCare.gov, Glossary. https://www.healthcare.gov/glossary/

Health Resources and Services Administration (HRSA). http://www.hrsa.gov/index.html

National Institutes of Health (NIH). http://www.nih.gov

National Library of Medicine, National Institutes of Health (NIH). *Medline Plus, Health Topics.* http://www.nlm.nih.gov/medlineplus/healthtopics.html

Schulte, Margaret F., *Healthcare Delivery in the U.S.A.: An Introduction, 2nd edition* (New York: Productivity Press, 2013).

U.S. Department of Health and Human Services (HHS). http://www.hhs.gov

## Additional References

Adams, Karen, and Janet M. Corrigan, eds., Committee on Identifying Priority Areas for Quality Improvement, Board on Health Care Services, Institute of Medicine. *Priority Areas for National Action: Transforming Health Care Quality* (Washington, DC: National Academies Press, 2003).

Advisory Board Company. *Three Key Elements for Successful Population Health Management.* http://www.advisory.com

Agency for Healthcare Research and Quality. http://www.ahrq.gov and https://cahps.ahrq.gov

American Academy of Physician Assistants. http://www.aapa.org

American Association of Medical Assistants (AAMA). http://www.aama-ntl.org

American Board of Medical Specialties (ABMS). http://www.abms.org

American Board of Professional Psychology (ABPP). http://www.abpp.org

American College of Emergency Physicians (ACEP). http://www.acep.org

American College of Physicians (ACP). https://www.acponline.org

American Health Information Management Association (AHIMA). http://www.ahima.org

American Medical Association (AMA). http://www.ama-assn.org/ama

Association of Academic Health Centers (AAHC). http://www.aahcdc.org

*CMIO Magazine.* http://www.cmiomagazine.com

Davidson, Stephen M. *A New Era in U.S. Health Care: Critical Next Steps under the Affordable Care Act.* (Stanford, CA: Stanford University Press, 2013).

Educational Commission for Foreign Medical Graduates (ECFMG). http://www.ecfmg.org

Enthoven, A.C. Integrated delivery systems: The cure for fragmentation. *Am J Manag Care* 15, 10 Suppl (2009): S284–S290.

HealthIT.gov. http://healthit.gov

Institute for Healthcare Improvement (IHI). http://www.ihi.org

Institute of Medicine. http://www.iom.edu

Iowa Hospital Association. *Common Health Care Abbreviations & Terminology* (Des Moines, IA: Iowa Hospital Association, 2008).

Joint Commission, The. http://www.jointcommission.org

Leapfrog Group, The. www.leapfroggroup.org

National Association of Clinical Nurse Specialists (NACNS). http://www.nacns.org

National Committee for Quality Assurance (NCQA). http://www.ncqa.org

National Home Infusion Association (NHIA). http://www.nhia.org

National Patient Safety Foundation (NPSF). http://www.npsf.org

National Quality Forum (NQF). http://www.qualityforum.org/Home.aspx

National Quality Measures Clearinghouse of the Agency for Healthcare and Quality. www.qualitymeasures.ahrq.gov.

National Research Corporation (NRC). http://www.nationalresearch.com

National Student Nurses Association (NSNA). http://www.nsna.org

Near Miss Registry. https://www.nearmiss.org

Pearson S.D., D. Goulart-Fisher, and T.H. Lee. Critical pathways as a strategy for improving care: Problems and potential. *Ann Intern Med.* 123 (1995):941–948.

SAMHSA (Substance Abuse and Mental Health Services Administration). *Leading Change: A Plan for SAMHSA's Role and Actions 2011–2014*, page 3, October 2010.

Urgent Care Association of America (UCAOA). http://www.ucaoa.org

U.S. Bureau of Labor Statistics. http://www.bls.gov

World Health Organization (WHO). http://www.who.int/en/